VOICES in the Juvenile Justice System

Clemens Bartollas
University of Northern Iowa

Stuart J. Miller
Washington & Jefferson College

PEARSON
Prentice Hall

Upper Saddle River, New Jersey 07458

10 9 8 7 6 5 4 3 2

ISBN 13: 978-0-13-225700
ISBN 10:   0-13-225700

CONTENTS

PREFACE

Voices in the Juvenile Justice System is made up of twenty-six stories. Sixteen of these stories are from youthful offenders, and ten stories have been contributed by individuals who are professionals in the justice system or agencies that work with youthful offenders. To provide a diverse collection of stories, the authors interviewed people from different parts of the United States; two were born in other countries.

These stories should be helpful in shedding light on those juveniles who commit illegal acts and are able to avoid involvement with the juvenile justice system and those juveniles who are processed in the juvenile system. Those stories contributed by professionals should be helpful in understanding the various roles, responsibilities, and approaches of those who work with juveniles in the justice system.

The stories are anonymous in the first part, but the authors are identified in the second selection of stories. Our intent is to protect the innocent; many of the stories in the offender section contain information that the writers would not want others to know.

It is the authors' hope that the substantive materials of the text will become alive when this material is illustrated in the context of individuals' lives. Some of these stories are quite painful and disturbing, while others are positive and even inspiring.

Acknowledgments

We are grateful to all of those who wrote their stories for this book. Michael Trimble, Eldria Brown, and Allyson Kolljeski transcribed, typed, and edited materials and kept the project moving.

Editor's Note

Although the interviews were edited for clarity, the Publisher and Authors would like to caution readers about the graphic subject matter and language within many of the stories in *Voices of Youthful Offenders and Professionals in the Juvenile Justice System*. Changing such subject matter and language would have resulted in a lack of authenticity and would have jeopardized the integrity of each story. This supplement is intended for mature audiences only.

PART I

YOUTHFUL
OFFENDERS

The stories in this section are contributed by individuals who have committed illegal acts when they were juveniles. Some of these individuals avoided apprehension by the police, while others were arrested at one time or the other. Nearly all of these individuals had drug histories of varying severity, and one of the stories illustrates how dangerous big-time drug trafficking can be. Several of the individuals experienced juvenile justice processing, including probation status and training school commitment. Two ended up in prison, and the third barely escaped a prison sentence in the spring of 2006.

DRUGS ARE COOL, MAN

I was raised by my mother, and I had a very happy childhood. I have a sister that is one year older than I am. My mom worked a factory job and sacrificed many of her personal wants to support us and ensure us a happy childhood. We lived in a decent neighborhood, and it was luxury compared to the inner city. I was a very good kid throughout elementary and middle school. Some people I knew started smoking pot and drinking alcohol in seventh and eighth grade, but I was still a straight arrow.

When I was in ninth grade, I had a serious girlfriend, but her brother happened to sell pot. (He is serving nine years in prison right now, go figure.) Well, one night he pulled me into a room and asked me if I would take a bag of pot over to his cousin who lived two blocks away from me. I felt cool, and I felt needed for this secret mission. When I got to the house, his cousin assumed I was going to smoke it, too. I was curious, so I did, and it was an escape from reality for a pampered fourteen-year-old. After that, I went over there every weekend, smoking pot and eventually drinking alcohol. I liked pot, but I loved drinking more.

By age sixteen, I was drinking three days a week, had lost my girlfriend, and lost contact with my good friends. Now I just had party buddies. I decided that it was time to move on. Not time to move on to other friends, but to move on to other drugs. I eventually tried every drug except heroin, because "that is only for real junkies." I was just experimenting, and it was harmless…right? WRONG! Alcohol and drugs can creep up on you and take control before you even realize. I was destroying my tight-knit family. My sister was my best friend, but now I just viewed her as a tattletale. To this day, the most depressing day of my life was when I was seventeen and my mom found a rolled-up dollar bill in my coat that I had used for cocaine. The tears rolled down her face, and I realized that I was in over my head, but I still did not stop.

I was attending alternative school by this time. I had been expelled from the main high school for my usual apathetic behavior. I needed to support my habit, so I decided to sell drugs for a short while. I sold some pot and once sold some bogus acid to kids. Luckily, they never found me. One of my best "friends" at the time was the object of obsession for the police department. His house got raided three separate times and robbed one other. I remember leaving the house one day while a car was pulling up. I didn't know the guys arriving, but I got a call a short while later saying that my friend had a gun pulled on him in his own house. I had escaped disaster every time, and I decided that I needed to change.

I changed to only drinking then, but drinking a lot. I crashed my car at age seventeen. I hit a parked car driving somebody home at one in the morning. I was arrested six hours later at seven o'clock in the morning and still had a blood alcohol level of 0.18. Everyone told me I was lucky to be alive. I decided to get smart and to not drink and drive, but to still drink (real smart, huh?). I was arrested again, for the second time, just six days later, but I still didn't learn my lesson. I pulled many more stunts that summer and ended up with six misdemeanors, including being a minor in possessions of alcohol, resisting arrest, and hindering and opposing a police officer. I stayed out of trouble for a brief period and graduated from my alternative school at age seventeen. After a short period of getting away with delinquent behavior, I got another MIP [Misdemeanor in Probation] and my second DUI. I spent twenty-five days in jail, and that was enough for me to turn my life around.

With the help of a loving mom, sister, uncle, and my new-found faith, I started attending a community college. After one year, I transferred to a university where I am close to finishing my undergraduate degree in Sociology.

How did a child with such a loving mother and sister get so turned around? What went wrong? Indeed, I caught many breaks, but I have still had to work extremely hard to get where I am right now. However, I will never forget who I was just four years ago. I plan to spend the rest of my life showing others that a life of crime is not a life one wants to live. Too many people continue down that beaten path, but hopefully I can show others that there is hope in turning their lives around.

Critical Thinking Questions

1. **How did someone with a grounded background get so deeply into the drug world?**

2. **How did this young man escape processing in the juvenile justice system?**

3. **Do you believe that his use of drugs reflects an addictive personality, or was it merely the influence of peers?**

4. **How did he turn his life around and stop his offending behaviors?**

I STARTED YOUNG

I moved to the state I live in now when I was two. My mom worked several jobs to be able to afford food and clothing for my sisters and me. When I was about five, she started to have frequent live-in boyfriends.

When I was seven, she met my step-dad, and he has been my dad ever since. My biological dad just did not care. I am the youngest of three. I lived on what you might call the "bad part of town."

I had a friend whose mom was heavily into drugs. When we were little, she would do them in front of us. She wouldn't let either of us do them, because we were just about seven at the time. She would openly do crank and speed. She would smoke marijuana in front of us. My friend came to my home one time in the middle of the night and said, "My mom is using a needle," and she wanted to come and stay at my place.

As I grew up, I realized exactly what my friend's mother was doing. I was in about fifth grade when my older sister who was about two years older started smoking and drinking. By sixth grade, I was smoking. That was before they put the cigarettes behind the counter. The cigarette stand was right next to the candy stand. My friends and I would go in; I would buy a candy bar, and they would grab a couple packs of cigarettes.

At the end of sixth grade, I got caught at the school with a carton and a half of Marlboro Reds in my backpack. I got kicked out of school for the last two or three weeks, but they didn't do any sort of legal thing with me then. They just took my cigarettes.

My mom wanted to know what the deal was. I said, "Everybody else smokes. So I do, too." My mom is a heavy smoker, and she was also an alcoholic. She did quit drinking a couple years ago. I grew up in a home where there was a lot of smoking and drinking. There was usually more beer in the fridge than there was anything for us kids.

When I got into seventh grade, I would snag beers out of the fridge without Mom knowing it. My mom was also very much into vodka, and she had bottles hidden throughout the house. She would forget about them. My friend and I would find them and get drunk.

My sister was doing marijuana at the time and LSD. She claimed that she only did crank five times. From ninth through eleventh grade, she said that she had done so much LSD that she got spacey. I always saw her getting high with her friends. I would stay in the room and talk with them. They always offered me some, but I would say, "I don't really want to do it myself. I'm only in seventh grade. I know I shouldn't do this."

By the time I was in ninth grade, I was doing pot all the time. From the time I was a freshman in high school until I got to college, I was high all the time. I took my SATs when I was purposefully high, just to see what would happen. I got so high that I almost forgot to go to school to take the test.

Drugs didn't really affect my grades. I was able to hold down my job. I never had to study for school; I was making B's and low B's while smoking pot all the time. I figured that if I cared enough to try harder, I could have done better. I never cared.

I was always the "go-to" girl when it came to drugs. If they needed drugs, they would come to me. And I would say, "Give me two minutes, and I will make a phone call." I would make a phone call, and a friend would say, "Let me call my dealer." Then I'd have the drugs in the next couple hours.

I was never the seller. I was like a little mule. I would get free drugs from doing this. I would also say, "When you use them, I get to share them with you."

At McDonalds, we would do drugs in the back room, especially on night shift. It wasn't uncommon for three or four people to do drugs. I would generally try to stick to the easier stuff, like weed. Some of the others did more serious stuff.

We would smoke four or five bongs at one setting. One time I was in a friend's garage where there was a box of his toys. There was a drum with a monkey on it, and all of a sudden this monkey was talking to me. I am sitting there, and it blew me out of my mind. I called my friend who was my go-to girl and wanted to know what was going on. She had a connection with her dealer. She said to her dealer, "What in the hell did you give us?" She said, "I thought you said that you wanted the P Special." She said, "No," and the dealer responded, "Well, what I gave you is laced with PCP." This was the best time I've ever gotten high, but it scared me out of my mind.

Out of all my childhood friends, I am the only one without a child. I have never been to rehab. All of my friends have been on probation. Four of my friends are currently in day treatment for drug use. My friend Jake got sent away, but I don't know where. He has been into heavy drugs, and for a while he was even into heroin and stuff like that.

The fact that I had a job also helped me get away from drugs. I was the only one of my friends who had a job, and I would volunteer to work Saturday nights because I knew that this was always the heaviest night of drug use. I knew that it was always Saturday night that they got busted.

My best friend just this past weekend was smoking meth. She said, "Do you want some?" I said, "No, I am good."

My boyfriend is heavily against drugs. I told him when we first started dating that I would never do drugs again. Even though it is really tempting, especially like at this time of the year when I am super stressed, I am staying away from them. I also know that if I were to get busted, I would lose everything I have worked for.

Critical Thinking Questions

1. Is it surprising that this young woman would get into smoking cigarettes and smoking marijuana given the background in her home and in her friend's home?

2. Why do you think that she has not become involved in the justice system as her friends have?

3. Would a person with this background make a good addiction counselor?

TRUAMA IN BOSNIA

I grew up in Bosnia, and I am an only child. My mother has had kidney problems. One of her kidneys doesn't work, and the other one only works about 30 percent. Before I was born, my mother had two miscarriages, and the doctors told her that if she tried to have kids again she would die. She decided to take the risk, get pregnant, and here I am.

My mom was a nurse, and my father was an anesthesiologist. Before the war, my mother started schooling to become a dentist, and she only had three more months of practice left. When the war started, she never finished the dental program.

The war began in 1992, and that is really what shaped my life. I was seven, but I remember everything that happened at the time. My best friend and I always hung out together. He was like my brother.   There was this big building by the hospital where doctors lived. Doctors got to live there for free, and that is where we lived. Right across the street was my best friend's house. His father worked as a paramedic, but his mother didn't work. He also was the only child they had.

On the evening of June 15, 1993, we were playing outside. I always had to tell my parents every hour of every day where we were in case the sirens would go off. They were constantly in the hospital because there were always wounded soldiers arriving.

We were outside playing. Around 5 pm. his mother came out and yelled to both of us to come inside and eat. We kept playing outside—the only two kids in the area—because we said we weren't hungry. There were guards there who knew my dad, and they always kept a close eye on us. I told him that I was going to tell my mom and dad where I am, and he said, "OK." Before I got to the hospital, I heard a sound in the air. It was like a whistling sound, like a grenade or bomb. So, I turned around, and his mother started to scream, "No," and a grenade falls right on the street in front of my best friend. It killed him.

I saw this, and I passed out. My parents were the first two people to come out. They heard the grenade and knew that we were the only two people outside. My mom came straight to me, and my dad went straight to him. My dad picked him up, and he didn't have any legs or arms. My dad started to run toward the hospital, and my friend died.

I was never at my friend's grave. I couldn't go to the funeral. No one ever told me where he was buried. They told me that it would be too hard for me to see his grave.

After that, I was in a kind of coma stage. Even when I woke up, I couldn't talk, and for three months I couldn't say a word. I never even tried; not even when I was by myself did I talk. No sound came out of my mouth. My parents took me to a specialist, and he said that he couldn't see anything wrong, but it might improve as time went by.

My best friend and I were together all the time. I would wake up at 6 am., and we would get together and watch cartoons. After he was gone, I felt that I had nobody. I would sit at my window and stare into a garden and cry. I didn't go to school; I didn't do anything. When any one came over, I would hide in my room. I didn't want to talk to anybody.

His mom and dad couldn't see me for three months. His dad started drinking a lot, and one night he came over. I was wrapped up in the long curtains in our living room; he came to our door and was crying. When I heard it was him, I ran up to him and started crying. I kept saying, "I'm so sorry. It is all my fault."

After that, I started to slowly begin to cope with it. In Bosnia, I didn't get into any trouble or anything. One of my other best friends lost his dad, and my dad had to take care of his family—his little brother and mom. It was a lot of stress on my dad. A lot of days my dad would not come home; he would be in the operating room at the hospital doing surgeries.

My dad started drinking a lot. When he started drinking, my grandmother who was a widower got worse. She used to come over and hit my mom, who couldn't defend herself, because she was so sick. Dad would be out drinking, and I would be home with my mom. Grandmother would tell my dad that my mom was sleeping around, and my mom was with me all the time.

I remember one time that my grandmother and my aunt came around and started to fight with my mom. I remember that they started to hit her in the kidneys. I ran out and yelled, "They're going to kill my mom; they're going to kill my mom." The neighbors came and got them off of her.

My mom got over all of that, but I haven't. My grandmother is in the United States now and has been diagnosed with lung cancer. She is a changed lady. But I can't get past what happened. Whenever I see her, what I see is how she was with my mom in Bosnia.

During the war, I remember that half of my childhood was spent in the basement. I couldn't go outside to play; for the four or five years of the war, I couldn't do anything. We didn't have electricity and had to use candles. I remember that I didn't have anything. Before the war, everything was wonderful, but once the war started, it was totally different. I moved seven times during the war because everything kept getting destroyed. I don't have a lot of baby pictures like most people have from their childhood; I really have nothing. There were people who starved to death because they really had nothing to eat.

There were a couple of the cities in Bosnia where the Serbs came into each of the houses, raped the women, killed the children, made the men watch, and killed them after that. The things that I saw were really sick. It has affected me in a lot of ways.

One day my dad came to me and said, "You've got to pack your stuff; we're going to the United States." I was nine.

When we came to the United States, we came with nothing. My parents told me to pack my bags, and I didn't know where we were going. The United States is a pretty big place. Later on, I found out where we were going.

Four days after coming here, I started school. I knew two words in English; I knew how to say "school," and I knew how to say "hello." On the first day of class, I cried to my father, "Please don't leave me," and he left me.

I got harassed in school, because I was the only foreign person. I came ten years ago. There was this kid Adam who always used to hit me and make fun of me because I couldn't say "green." That really scared me for life. I would cry all day, but I didn't know how to say to the teacher, "He just hurt me. He just hit me."

I felt so handicapped. That's the feeling you have. You don't know anything; you don't know where to go. You went through hell in the war, and so you come to even more hell. Even though you are safe and can go outside, what are you going to do outside when you don't know anybody.

I learned English, and by seventh grade, I started to be popular. The thing that hurts me about my life story is that my parents did everything to raise me right. They came here so that I could have a better future; we could have stayed, because the war ended two months after we came here.

Everything I have done I regret because of them. I started to smoke cigarettes in seventh grade with girls who were my friends. My best friend was a really, really bad girl. Her mom has had three hundred boyfriends and so forth. When I got into eighth grade, I started hanging out with even worse kids, and I started smoking weed. I got a boyfriend who used to do drugs. I started to hang out with him, and I felt that I had nothing else to live for. I had nothing to lose. I felt that throughout my whole life I had been screwed.

I started to hang out with a couple of boys who did heavy drugs. I'm glad that I never did everything that they did, and I'm glad that I turned some of their drugs down. I smoked weed with them. They also used to steal cars. I was there as the lookout and what not.

Throughout this time, I would lie to my parents. I would tell them that I was going one place when I was going some place different.

Then, my boyfriend started to do ecstasy. I went to this party and started drinking. He said, "You should do this." I took one and tried it. It was the worse thing I've ever experienced. After that, I came home. My mom said, "What's going on with you?" I said, "I'm tired; I'm going to bed."

My parents always pushed me to do good in school, but my grades started dropping. I always felt that I wasn't good enough for them, and I had always let them down. I had always screwed up, so I might as well keep doing it.

When I hit high school, I started skipping school and hanging out with my friends. We were smoking and drinking. My sophomore year I got kicked out of school. I had this sociology and psychology teacher who really liked me, and he went to the principal and said, "You guys just don't understand. This girl is bright; she is hanging out with bad people. Try to let her come back to school."

All the teachers went and talked with the principal, and my mom and cried and begged, "Please don't kick her out of school." My parents didn't know how much I had missed school, because I had people call in for me.

They let me back in school. The told me, "This is your last chance. If you screw it up, you're out."

Then, a couple weeks after that, I got kicked out again. I was sitting in history class, and my teacher stood up and said, "I know what it was like for those Bosnians to come here." He kept saying that he knows what it's like. I was sitting there and said, "No, you don't; I don't really think you should be talking s--- like this." He said to me, "You need to watch your mouth." I said, "You need to watch your mouth, too. You just can't sit up here and tell everybody you know. You say it like a joke, like there aren't dead people here and there. You don't know what it's like. You spent your childhood here, watching cartoons. You never had to sit in a basement for three months, with no electricity or food."

The teacher said, "You need to get out of my class." I said, "Whatever," and they told me, "You're done." I went back to my psychology teacher, and my parents came. The people that sponsored my aunt and uncle from the Methodist church, and my aunt and uncle then sponsored us – they came, and they spoke up for me.

I went home, and my parents said, "You're going to Bosnia." They sent me to Bosnia for two months to live alone. I found out where my best friend was buried, and I spent most of my time there, just thinking that I could have ended up like this. Something made me survive, and I felt that my best friend was looking down on me. That trip to Bosnia was the biggest change in my life. I then realized everything. I thought, "My God, what am I doing?"

So, the night that I came back, all of my friends that I used to hang around with came around to see me. I opened the door and just stood there. I thought that this is not what I want to do. I told them, "I'm sorry, but I'm busy."

That is when I started to be really close to my parents. I went back to high school. I told them, "I want to finish two years in one," and they let me do it. I had all A's my last year of high school; I went to college and was the valedictorian of my two-year program in community college.

I am determined to make my people proud. I want to show the people around me that Bosnians can do something here. We get discriminated against, too. You don't know how many times I have heard, "Why don't you go back to your own country? You don't belong here." I have been lucky through all of the things I've done that I don't have a record. It could have been a lot worse.

Critical Thinking Questions

1. How did the specific events of the war witnessed by this person affect her?

2. Is it surprising that she would get into peer groups that did, in her words, "bad things"?

3. What impact did visiting her friend's grave in Bosnia have on her? Do you think it would have been less traumatic for her to have been able to visit his grave following his death?

4. What does the story of her life have to say about the resilience of the human spirit?

THE DAY THEY TOLD ME I COULD GO FREE WAS THE END OF TROUBLE FOR ME

There was not a lot of stability throughout my adolescence. I was born in Austin, Texas. I lived and commuted back and forth from Austin, Miami, and Los Angeles. My mother had hopes of getting back with my father (her ex-husband). At that time, he lived in the Midwest. We came to the Midwest, and it was completely different there. We stayed with my dad, and three or four months into it my dad beat my mom. I was ten years old at the time. My mother left my dad, and we were forced to live in a shelter. We stayed there for about seven or eight months.

From there we moved to where I live now, and I was enrolled into elementary school. Although there was a lot of stability in my elementary years, I did have to deal with a few problems. One was racism; there were very few minorities in the school I attended. At times it was hard to hear what others were saying about me. I had never dealt with racism before.

Another memorable moment in my childhood was when someone very close to my family got into trouble with the law. I was labeled because of what happened from that situation. So, from the eighth grade on, I was labeled as a troublemaker and as gang-related because I had a lot of older guys who I looked up to. They were like big brothers to me, since I had no older role model for myself. I was talking to Vice Lords and Gangster Disciples, and they saw me as a good kid. They did want me to join their family or gang. For some reason, I chose not to join their gangs, but I still associated with them. At this same time, my brother, my mom, and I were in and out of court due to the instance that came about in my seventh-grade year with a family member.

I went through high school in the town I live in now. My younger brother followed me in high school. At the end of my senior year, somebody that was extremely close to me and my brother went to jail. This was at the time when my brother was in the transition of going from high school to college. He was going to go to a local Division I college, and he had a full ride scholarship to play football there. So, it was very hurtful for us because we were associated with this person.

When this close friend of mine was in jail, I guess you could say that I was not very "civil." I ended up getting into a fight. I hit this kid a couple of times, and he went ahead and pressed charges against me. They wanted to charge me with a class D felony. I was in and out of court for that. They were trying to give me five years for this situation. At the last meeting before we went to trial, the judge took me to the side and told me that they were going to offer me a plea bargain one last time. It was to spend thirty days at Oakdale [a prison in Iowa]. I asked the judge if I could have a couple days to think about it, but he told me that I had to decide now. So, my choice was to accept the plea bargain and try to get out of Oakdale in thirty days or try my luck with a jury (which meant I could spend up to five years in prison). I thought about it and took the deal.

I tell you what – I will never forget that experience in this lifetime. It was equivalent to

Hell, if you ask me. When I was in jail, I told myself that I was going to turn my life around. I wanted to be a good citizen for society. After two weeks of being there, I went ahead and started helping people that were locked up. It made me feel better that I was helping others.

On the thirtieth day, I called my family to tell them that I was ready to get out and asked them if everything was OK outside the walls. It turned out that it was not. They informed me that the judge who was supposed to set me free went on vacation. This crushed me. I had counted down the days, and to have this come down on me like that felt like it was crushing me. I prayed so much to get out.

On the night of the thirtieth day, they called my name out. I was being transported to another prison. I thought, "How could they do this to me?" I put all my heart and soul into getting out and helping others, and then they do this to me. They chained me up and put me on the bus. I had no idea where I was going, but I knew it couldn't be good. The first stop was Fort Dodge. They call this the "gladiator camp" because this is where all the young troublemakers go. I thought to myself, "Well, I guess this is home". The bus driver said, "If I say your name get off the bus; if I don't, stay on the bus." The guy went through all of the names and never read mine. I had no idea what was going on; it felt like I was in a movie or something. He told us that the next stop was Rockwell. When I saw the camp, it was like there was music in my ears. It was much more free than at Oakdale. It was like some of my prayers came true because I wasn't in my cell twenty-three hours a day. At Rockwell, we could be outside all day. One day they called my name over the PA system, and I went to see what was up. This is the time that they informed me I was approved to be set free, and it was an amazing feeling to have. Moreover, that was the end of trouble for me.

Critical Thinking Questions

1. **Should this young man have gone to prison?**

2. **Should this young man have been treated as he was by the system?**

3. **What lessons does this story teach us about handling youngsters, especially those who have a lot of problems in their backgrounds?**

4. **What do you think about the judge going on vacation when he had promised this young person that he would be released, if he had good behavior the thirty days he was confined?**

PEERS CREATED SOME GRIEF FOR ME

I am from a small town, and we are middle class. My parents work for a living. I have a sister but no brothers. I moved around a lot when I was very little. We lived in seven towns before I was the age of ten. We finally settled into the town where I ended up growing up. I went to a really small school.

I did well in school. I graduated seventh in my class. I never really had any problems in school. I didn't even drink, smoke, or do drugs.

I got involved my freshman and sophomore years in high school with a peer group that most people would regard as not the coolest kids. The "dirty kids," I guess I would say. After my sophomore year, I began to get more involved in extracurricular activities. So, I would say that I began to hang out with more "popular kids." I was also homecoming queen. I was in drama, so I was in all of the school plays.

I had problems with the justice system three times. The first time, I was sixteen. What happened was a couple of friends came to pick me up in a car that was not theirs. It was a brand new white truck, really nice, and I knew it was not theirs. I had no clue where they got it. I got in, and they told me that they had stolen it. I didn't get out; I stayed in. I was just really surprised that they had gone and stolen this truck.

Needless to say, the people who had their truck stolen reported it. We got pulled over and taken out of the car, with guns drawn and the whole works. I was really scared; I had a gun pointed at my head. I was only sixteen years old. The police only took the driver and passenger in the front seat to the police station. Luckily, I was in the back seat. They interrogated me for a while and ended up just letting me go. That was the first time.

The second time wasn't as bad, I guess. I was at a party that was busted. The police officers did not feel that giving us all possession tickets was bad enough punishment, so they arrested five of us and made us go to jail. This was my first time in jail. We just got a possession, which later ended up getting dropped.

The third time, nine of my friends and I broke into the school the day after my high school graduation. This was our senior prank that got a little out of hand. Somebody saw us break into the school. We broke a lock on a window to get in. We had a lookout person outside of the school to see if any cops were driving by. Well, our lookout person called, and by that time it was too late. The school was completely surrounded. So, we ran down to the basement and hid in a tiny crawl space for three hours until they finally found us. I was very scared because it was dark and we could hear the officers searching through the school. They finally yelled into the tunnel and said that if anyone was in there they better come out or they were going to send in the dogs, and we could hear the dogs barking. So, we crawled out of the tunnel. This was the second time I had a gun drawn on me. This time they arrested all of us. They took us to jail, but this time I was charged as an adult because I was eighteen. They interrogated me for about two hours, and I was charged with burglary. The whole court appearance process took about four months, but in the end I got a deferred judgment. I was very lucky.

I have thought a little bit about why I did what I did. The last time, the school incident, I did it because I did not want to miss out on anything. I thought that if I didn't do it, then people would call me a baby or chicken, so I went ahead and did it. I thought it would be cool if we had got away with it to see the reaction we got. The time our party got busted, I never really thought anything of it beforehand. I knew there was a chance of us getting busted, but we have had parties and got away with it before, so I just took a chance.

Critical Thinking Questions

1. **What would motivate an adolescent who was doing so well in school and did not drink, smoke, or do drugs to become involved in these three incidents?**

2. **Do you believe that the juvenile and, later, the adult justice system handled her properly for her violations?**

3. **If she had had more offenses in her background, had been male, or had been a member of a minority, do you believe that her case would have been handled differently?**

I COULD BE IN DEEP TROUBLE NOW

I was born in Silsbee, Texas. I was there until I was a freshman in high school. My relationship with my mother was real good. I have two younger brothers. My father was around until I was five, but then my mother met Ray.

I was in the fourth grade, and my two younger brothers were also in school. I was going to walk my youngest brother (who was in kindergarten) to school, but my mom said she would do it. We got back home after school and saw all these ambulances at our house. We didn't know what was going on. We saw this woman lying on the ground and didn't think anything of it. We went inside our house and found out that our mother had been shot. We didn't know who would do such a thing.

We found out later that it was Ray. It all started two days previous to the shooting. His father had passed away four years before this happened. In the past, whenever they would get into a fight, my grandpa would come over and settle things down. So now, whenever they would get into a fight, my mom didn't have anyone to help her out. She began to drink more because of this. She and Ray also did crack together.

After she was shot, my brothers and I had to go through a process where they wanted us to become a ward of the State. I was so confused because I wanted to go with my real dad. The sad thing was that we had our grandma and aunts who wanted to take care of us, but they wouldn't let it happen. It's not like my mother was a bad parent; she just made a bad choice by staying with Ray. My mother stayed in the hospital for about a week.

I went back to school the following week, and on the second day I was taken to the principal's office to talk to some officers. They told me I needed to go with them. I was young; I had no idea what was going on. They took me to a youth shelter. When I got there, my younger brothers were already there. My youngest brother was very scared and crying, so I had to make him feel better by telling him that everything was going to be all right. Even though at that time, I had no idea what was going on. I was ten at this time. We stayed there for two weeks. We were wondering why we could not see our mom. We didn't understand the situation. We ended up being in foster care for about seven months.

The foster parent situation was kind of weird. They split my middle brother up, but kept my little brother and me together. This messed up my relationship with my middle brother. They took him to another town in Texas to be to be with a foster family. We finally got to go back to my great-grandmother, which is my mother's grandmother. This was a lot better, since our mother lived right down the street from there.

I started to get in trouble in sixth grade, I started hanging out with these kids. Our favorite movie was "Colors," and we started copying what the movie portrayed. We would go to the dollar store and buy a pack of bandanas for a dollar. I never really joined a gang, but I hung out with them. Plus my great grandma told me never to join one.

The first thing that I did was not that major, but at the time to us it was. We would stay out really late and break the curfew. We would sneak out our windows and have the cops chasing us all of the time. We hated the cops. We thought that they were just out to get us.

It was at that point that we started to rob and steal cars. I am not going to get into that, but it is stupid to steal a car. My middle brother is locked up now for stealing cars. He wanted to be a Crip. He got tattoos and all that stuff. I wasn't going to do all that. I got tattoos too, but they aren't associated with gangs. His whole thing was that his dad was in prison, and he wanted to be like his dad. They do have very similar qualities. He is in and out and in and out of correctional facilities. He has been locked up since he was fifteen. He is twenty now.

The next thing that happened is I ran into Big Gun. Big Gun was a guy in the neighborhood that we all looked up to. He was like a 6-foot 9-inch guy that played basketball in high school. He could have gone anywhere, but he wanted to sell drugs and be the black Scar Face of the neighborhood. This was the guy that we all looked up to because he had a car. He had a TV in his car. He did have a lot of girlfriends, too. We always wanted to be like this guy; he was cool. We didn't know that he was trying to use us.

That is what happened with the backpack thing. I lived three blocks from Big Gun, and he had these big old thick backpacks. They had pouches on them. He would tell us to go knock on a door and leave the pouches. "OK, Big Gun." We never looked in the pouches, and we got $100. We'd buy video games with the money. We did that for probably four months before we looked in the pouches. My cousin, Marcus, said, "What's this white stuff? Candy, sugar, what?" So Marcus tastes it.

That is when his mother found out and called my mother. My mother said that she was going to take us to talk Big Gun. We were scared to death to talk to him. My mom is 5-foot 11, but she can still handle herself. I told my mom that he would kill her! I didn't want her involved with him. Marcus's mom said she was going to call the police and tell them about the package. She did give it back to him, but she took pictures of what was in it. My mom talked to him, but Big Gun didn't think it was too big of a deal.

Up until my freshman year, everything was all right. But, that is when Marcus got shot over some stupid stuff. It didn't kill him, but it messed him up bad. It was a gunshot in the back! He was trying to steal a radio from this guy. Why? I don't know. We kept trying to tell him, "What are you going to do with the radio? You aren't going to make much money from it."

I did my share of stealing. This girl and me were always going to Wal-Mart to get the little return tags. We would walk in like we had something in the sack. I would walk around while she went and got something. She would go get a CD player, and we would steal it. You could get $39 from those CD players.

Another scheme is that we would go to the pawnshop. Our parents would buy things for us, and we would pawn them. The problem was that we weren't eighteen, so we would find kids from the neighborhood and give them $5 if they would pawn something for us. That was another thing that made my mom so mad. I was probably doing it to make sure I had money. When you are in eighth grade and you have money, the girls like it. That is why I did it.

My uncle is a policeman. I thought he sold out. I was a little ninth grader and saw people get beat up by the police because they were tied up in gangs. I would say to him, "You suck. You are supposed to be from here. What is wrong with you? Why are you a police officer?" He never argued with me. He just said, "One day you will realize." "No, I will not," I said.

I know that if I would have stayed in school I wouldn't have done anything. What was going on was right in our neighborhood. There was no point in going to school. I did have problems with eighteen-, nineteen-, and twenty-year-olds in the neighborhood trying to beat me down. I looked much older, even though I was not. My mom used to always tell me that they didn't want to see me succeed because they knew I had talent. They were stuck there, so they wanted to make me stuck, too. They were my friends, so I didn't care about all of that.

Then I started wearing red and white, the gang colors. I never really joined the Bloods, but it would signify my relationship with them. I would get stopped by the police! I still wear my red t-shirts and stuff like that today. I am not in a gang.

There was a shooting one time. This is what really made my mom mad. I was walking down the street with my red T-shirt, hat, and shoes after football practice. The police drove up to me and swooped me in the car. I was trying to resist because I was innocent. That was my first case. They didn't take me down to the station, but to the juvenile detention center. I was in there with crazy kids, with people who really shoot kids and steal money. They just thought I was a gang member. I was in there for two days without talking to anybody. They were going to take me to jail. I was fifteen years old and didn't have an ID. They thought I was twenty-one, but they wouldn't believe me. I wasn't saying anything at first. I said that I didn't associate with gangs. This detective asked me why I was wearing those colors. I said that they were in my neighborhood; I told him that you don't understand. I said, "This is like jail, right, I get a phone call." "No, you don't," he said. "You get a hearing after being in here for a day or two."

The whole time I was in there, I decided that I couldn't do this. I couldn't. I looked around and saw how it was. There were three beds, five people, a toilet, and a sink. I knew that these were guys who had killed people. I started thinking about what my uncle was saying. Prison would be worse; this is how bad it could be.

I was in there just because I lived in the neighborhood. Some guys end up in jail because they are associated with a gang. Some guys kill in jail just because they don't want anyone else in there. I sat down with this one little kid. He was fat and younger than me. He was talking about killing and how it wasn't no big deal. Finally my mom came, and I said, "You got to get me out of here. I want to finish the semester."

My mom moved to Oklahoma. I was going back and forth between my mom and father. The only problem was I didn't get along with my dad's wife at times. I didn't like her. She was a prissy lady. She always said that guys should wear their hair short, but I didn't. My dad would let her say anything she wanted to say, and I didn't like that. I didn't really want to stay with either of them.

The guys in Oklahoma thought they were tough, and they belonged to a fake gang. They were nothing. Oklahoma City was another thing. There were a lot of bad things that went on in that city. We were an hour and a half away. When we got our licenses, we went to Oklahoma City. There were a lot of people acting stupid there. We saw two guys get shot. This was my first time I saw somebody get shot. It was weird.

Another incident took place in school. Coming from an all-black school to a school where there were whites was a little strange. First, I didn't know what "gothic" was. They had trench coats on, wore makeup, and were very different. They were outcasts; I didn't want to be like that. I was more scared of them than someone who was known to stab somebody. The administration created an alternative school for the "bad" kids. This was called "Teen Academy." You could do one thing at this school and be sent there.

I was almost sent there once, but never made it. This took place when this guy thought that I was trying to get with his girlfriend. I had heard that he was talking about me, so I went to find him. Where I come from, you don't say things about another person. When I saw him, my first reaction was to punch him. He was the so-called man in sports until I got there. We worked it out without fighting.

There was another incident, and it became a big thing. We broke into an old house. Listening to my stupid friends led me to do this. They were smoking weed; I had never smoked before. I had tasted alcohol, but never smoked weed. So, we were sitting around smoking and got the idea to break into this old house. We didn't steal anything, just looked around. On our way out of the house, a lady saw us. We thought nothing of it. The next weekend we were sitting around smoking again and got another crazy idea to break into one of our friend's houses who was out of town. We broke in, and it was one of them silent alarm things. We were all high as a kite, and the cops showed up. They took no mercy on us, threw us on the floor, and cuffed us. They took us to jail.

I called my uncle to come and get me. He told me that he wasn't going to come and get me. He told me that I needed to stay there for a while. This really made me angry. I never thought I was going to be in jail, even though I was raised in a bad environment. Here I was "in jail."

The judge made me do community service. I had to go to the junk yard every Saturday morning for six months. I also had to write a paper to the city apologizing for what I had done. I also had to do counseling, which I thought was all bull. I was afraid that everyone would look at me as a "criminal."

It all ended up working in my favor. I got a football scholarship to the University of Oklahoma. I just look back at all of the times I could have got into trouble, and I am thankful for what has happened to let me get this far.

Critical Thinking Questions

1. Should this young person have been processed further into the justice system?

2. What could have been done for him when he was younger that would have been a constructive force in his life?

3. Why did he flirt with, rather than become, deeply involved with gangs?

4. How important was his uncle to this young person?

I AM JUST A SMALL TOWN GIRL

I grew up on a farm and in a rural setting. I went to a very small public school. Everything was normal until we were in sixth grade and Helen Reddy sang the song, *I Am Woman.* A number of the girls in my class really listened to the song and took it to heart. I remember we would sing this song, and it became sort of a mantra. At the same time, the Vietnam War was in progress, and it was a different time.

One way it affected me was in tenth grade around Christmastime. We were riding around in a car, probably doing some drinking. We saw this big Santa that lights up sitting on a porch. We decided to take it. We put it in the trunk of the car. It was around 11 pm. With this success, we went around town stealing Christmas lights. We had a trunk full of Christmas lights by the time it was all done. We took them back to a friend's house who lived right in town and put them on the living room floor. "Wow," we felt, "we really achieved something."

I remember her brother and friend were up, and they said, "What are you doing?" I remember thinking that there really was not anything wrong with this. We didn't make a connection with stealing. So, I went home.

On Monday or Tuesday, we were called individually into the superintendent's office. I lied and said that I didn't know what they were talking about. Several of us lied. I was not punished; the ones who admitted to it were punished. I can't remember what the punishment was, but the juvenile courts were not involved. I know why I lied; I was playing sports, and I didn't want to be kicked off the team. I didn't want to give up my entire basketball season.

There was another time that we, and this was a different group of girls, spray painted all around town. We sprayed painted in front of the school, at the public park, and other places. It was big. I didn't get caught on this either, but I am sure they were suspicious.

I smoked cigarettes occasionally as a juvenile. I never carried them. We just did it from time to time. Alcohol was more my thing. We had a lot of underage drinking parties.

I began to smoke some pot at the end of my high school years. One of my friends' brothers was in a band, and she got the pot from him. She started smoking it, and another girlfriend and I smoked it with her. My senior year we smoked pot quite a bit. It started out as a weekend thing, but I remember several times we were high when we went to school. It wasn't an everyday thing, though, and we never got caught.

Later on, following high school, I did get caught. I was going to cosmetology school and this guy that I met and didn't really know very well said to me, "Do you want to go smoke a joint?" I said, "Yeah, sure." We went out to the parking lot, and no sooner had we lit up the cops were there. They took me down to city hall and booked me. I was scared. That was a turning point for me. They allowed me to walk home; I wasn't pressed with any charges because they had thrown the evidence out.

Also, following high school, I went beyond pot. I did Quaaludes, acid, and coke, and I did mushrooms once.

The only time I have been in the system was sixteen years ago when I was charged with a DWI. I was in my late twenties and spent a night in jail. It was horrible. It took me another year or two to decide never to drink again and to stay away from everything. But it was a huge turning point because I have not had alcohol or used anything else for thirteen years.

I have come to realize that there was an addictive pattern there all along. My parents kept pointing it out. At first, I was pretty defensive about it. It didn't consume my life, and I was lucky in a lot of ways. It was more of an experiment or something to do. I was probably a little farther out than a lot of the others, but it seemed to be OK.

There are other people out there who do have similar patterns or problems. I think I was lucky because of the time period. I would probably be looked upon as a juvenile delinquent if it happened today, and I would end up in the system. Yet I don't necessarily regret any of my past experiences because I do believe I am a better person because of them. I also am able to understand others who have addictions.

Critical Thinking Questions

1. **Why do you think Helen Reddy's song, *I Am Woman,* had such an effect on these rural girls?**

2. **Why would rural girls become involved in the capers described in this story and become so involved in pot smoking?**

3. **If an adolescent's addictive pattern is discovered by parents or other social control agents, what could be done that would be more helpful to the adolescent?**

ABUSIVE TREATMENT IN MORE THAN ONE CULTURE

I was born in India. My home in India would be Channai, but the British changed it to Madras. My mother and father, who are from India, owned a liquor store in India, and we were in the low caste. I had two older brothers and one younger brother and sister. I don't really have much memory of my older brothers because they married and moved away.

When I was about three or four my father died of a kidney or liver problem. But it could have been prostate disease. I do remember one day when he couldn't pee, and at that time I was mad at him because he wouldn't go get me candy. He would put me on his shoulder and go get me candy all the time. Anyway, he died, and I really didn't know what the meaning of death was because I was so young. I believed for the longest time that I was the one who killed him because I threw rocks at him that day because he wouldn't get me candy.

I remember quite a bit of the funeral. He was getting cremated. I remember trying to run up there, but somebody held me back from getting burned. I was telling everybody not to burn my dad. I just wish I didn't remember half of this stuff, but I have a very good memory. That's the problem. I can remember the events that go on in my life and other people's lives. I can remember what somebody else did at a certain time, and they don't even remember it.

As time went on, I was about six years old and my little brother was four. I used to remember following my mom to every job she had. She had to work like three or four jobs, and one of her jobs was at a military base as a cook. I remember following her, and when she saw me, she slapped me on the butt and told me to go home. I said, "I think you should stay home so I can work." Even though I was six years old, I felt like I was the man. I think I was mature for my age. Not a day goes by that I don't think of these memories. I don't mean to dwell on them, but they were so traumatic to me.

A couple of months later my mother decided that she could only take care of one of us. My little sister was the baby, so she kept the baby and put me and my brother in an orphanage. I didn't want to be in an orphanage, and I acted out and got in trouble. They put me in a really, really bad kid orphanage. At the time I was about six and a half and my brother was about four and a half. They kept my brother in the Concord House of Jesus for the good kids and put me with the bad kids. I was acting up because I was angry from being taken from my home. I didn't know how else to react to it except cause a lot of trouble around the orphanage were I was at. The orphanage couldn't control me either, so they just sent me back to the Concord House of Jesus.

Every kid was beaten there, but there were times when me and my brother were beaten with bamboo sticks, bike chains, and belts. No sexual s--- ever went on in my life. It was always physical and mental pain.

When Americans came to adopt a kid from the orphanage, they usually bought gifts for the kids that were there. The caretakers would take them after the Americans left, and they would lock them up in a cabinet. My little brother was able to figure out how to break into the cabinet. He would break in, and he would get all the toys out. He would give them to all the kids. He and me were kind of like Robin Hood and Little John. I was little John, and he was Robin Hood. My brother, who, being a sneaky little s---, figured that since I was the oldest and the biggest, I'll take all the beatings while he did all the crimes and stuff. It kind of became a little one-two punch. So all the s--- that happened there was because we were trying to fight the system. If something was not fair in the orphanage, kids would come to my brother and me, and we would take care of it.

I just became immune to the beatings that I would laugh half the time. I remember one time when they tried to hit me with a bamboo stick, and I grabbed the stick and broke it on my knee. I just threw it at the caretaker. For some reason, they just kept backing away from me because they thought they might have created a monster. They started to leave my brother and me alone about stuff.

We were supposed to be adopted by this family in Washington, and it fell through because they were sick and tired of waiting for the adoption papers. We felt like we were abandoned. We knew we were getting to the age where we were kind of getting too old to be adopted; I started to become depressed.

I don't know if it was good or bad, but we were adopted by a family in Kansas. They would send us pictures, toys, and all that stuff. We were very thankful that they wanted to adopt two abandoned kids. The day before my adopted parents came to take us to America, they let us see our mom. That was probably the one thing that still keeps me in a sad state every night. They pretty much had to pull me away from my mom, because I didn't want to let go.

So we were adopted by this family from Kansas. We came to America on June 8, 1991. We really didn't know how to speak English at all. The thing was, we learned pretty fast. We went to a tutor every morning, except Sundays, during the summer because school started in August, and we came in June. So we knew how to carry on a normal conversation by the time school rolled around, but we couldn't read well. I still am a slow reader, but I comprehend well. There were times when my brother and me were mad and we started bitching at them in our language.

They had two daughters who were fourteen and fifteen at the time, and they had an adopted kid from Thailand who was four. I was eight and my brother was six. We never felt that we were loved because they knew what happened in India. They knew all the stuff that went on because they were informed through the papers and stuff about how to deal with us. Every time my brother or I would lie, there would be a big beating. We were the only two that got spanked, but the two girls loved us like we were their own brothers.

My adopted parents didn't know how to deal with us. My brother and me would lie about stuff so we wouldn't get in trouble. There were times, like when my brother knocked over a lamp and broke it, he lied about it because that boy had more fear in him than anything else. I was the opposite because I didn't have any fear. There was this one time that we were starting to speak English a little better, but every time we spoke in our language we would get a beating because they wanted to Americanize us.

The wife was worse. I called the husband my ex-dad. He was about 190–195 pounds and 6-feet tall, and my ex-mom was about 150 pounds and 5-foot eight. So they weren't small. They were morally good people, but they just didn't know how to react to the s--- that my brother and me had gone through.

It was really dark in the house, and we were trying to become familiar with where everything was in the house. My brother accidentally walked into the closet and started peeing. The next morning my ex-parents came down to wake us up to go to church. They smelled pee, and they went into the closet. There was pee in it.

They knew I didn't do it because I never had any bladder problems, but my brother did. He always has to go to the bathroom. I said it wasn't me, and Kyle said that it wasn't him, and I ended up getting a smack across the face. Then they smelled my brother's PJs, and they had pee all over them. She jumped on him when he was in his bed. She was sitting on him and started beating him. I'm just sitting there full with rage. I was just too little to do anything. She puts a pillow over his head and tells him to stop screaming. She lifted it off and continued to hit him. Then that ended, and we all went to church.

My ex-sisters tried to stay out of it. It was almost like they were real sisters. To tell you the truth, half this s--- happened when they weren't even around. They would have got into it because they kept getting angry every time something happened to us.

Time went on, and the same s--- continued. When I was about eleven or twelve, that was the last time I got a beating because I got too big. I remember the last time well My ex-dad sat on me and just kept punching me in the face. I became so damn immune to this that I just built a steel wall around my face. I just have so many scars here and there.

My temper had got to the point where it just started growing bigger and bigger, waiting for one day to explode. After I got the beating, I took the air pump and was just messing around with it. I took the air compressor, and I put it in my mouth. I was just messing around to see what it felt like. My sisters were babysitting us that day; one told me to stop doing that because it's bad for you. I stopped doing it, but my sisters told my parents when they came home. They didn't think anything would happen. And then my ex-dad comes over, winds up, and smacks me right on the nose and mouth at the same time. My nose started bleeding. He said, "Your nose is bleeding because you put that air compressor in your mouth." I looked at him and said, "No, you just hit me." He started to hit me again. And then I gave him the dirtiest look possible. He stopped.

In school I was doing good because I started picking everything up really fast. School was no problem, and I got along with my peers well. When I was about twelve or thirteen, I started hanging out with the bad kids, but I never caused any trouble. I could relate to them because they got the same s--- going on in their house as I did. The teachers would tell my ex-parents that I'm hanging out with the bad kids. Then I would get beatings for it. I did dread parent-teacher conferences because the teachers would say one hundred good things about me, and then they would say, but he has a hard time sitting still in class because he has ADHD.

One morning I was sitting there eating cereal, and my brother was standing by the radio singing a song. My ex-dad came in and said, "What are you doing?" He said, "Nothing." My ex-dad accused him, "Why are you lying to me? I heard you singing." He grabs my brother by the throat and throws him against the door. I still was not big enough yet. I looked at him and said, "Don't touch my brother." He comes over, and he smacks me across the face. I looked at him and said, "Your time's coming, old man." And then he gave me another punch. I just got to the point where all I was doing was being a smart ass. I would go to him and say, "You can ground me. You can beat me; you can do whatever you what, but you aren't going to faze me. I'm immune to this s---. You aren't going to break me."

When I was about sixteen and my sisters were both graduated from college, I got my first job at McDonalds. I was working overtime and came home late. She started bitching at me, and I said, "Why can't you just let me come home and sit here a little bit before you start your bitching?" She looked at me and said, "The only bitch was your bitch birth mom." That was it. I looked at her and said in a calm way, "You can't expect us to love you guys more than we love our real parents. You can never expect that. You have never been the number-one parents in our lives. And my mom is not a bitch; you are a f------ bitch." I had sworn at them before, but I never called her a f------ bitch before.

She went to get her husband. She told him what I said, and he hit me in my jaw. There was a couch behind me, and I fell over the couch. Then I stood up again with the cockiest smile and adjusted my jaw from left to right. I threw an elbow at his face and knocked him out cold. Knocked him out cold. He woke up and said, "Pack your stuff. You're leaving."

I packed my stuff up and went to my best friend's house. We went to court and all that stuff. We had to wait until I was eighteen to be out of their custody, but I didn't have to live with them. I was put in a foster home. What was funny about the foster family is I had gone to high school with their daughter, who was a year older than me. They knew about me, and they knew my story and stuff.

The trouble began again, right around the time when the girl who I was going to date died. She had heart surgery, and then right after that she got the flu and her heart couldn't fight it. I started getting into fights and all that stuff. I started missing work, and then they put me in a boy's home for about two or three weeks. That's where I pretty much decided that I didn't want to go that route. I didn't want to be a troublemaker. I wanted to be who I am. I wanted people to see me and what I was doing was not me. How I kept getting into trouble and fights was not me.

I wanted to divorce my adopted parents because they still had custody over me since I wasn't eighteen yet. But then my lawyer and my foster parents said it would be better if they didn't terminate rights because I still needed the insurance. With the courts, I found out that if I lived independently I would have never had any help with school and stuff.

One day I actually ran away from my foster parents' house, and they had no idea where I was. Then I came back home. My foster mom was like a second mom to me besides my real mom. She started crying. She hugs me, and then she slaps me and said, "Don't do that to us again." They loved me like a son. So I didn't have the right to do that to them because they had never done nothing but give me good hospitality and show me what good people are about.

There was a police lady sitting there who lectured me, "You shouldn't have done that to them. They really love you and were worried about you." My foster father was a cool cat. I wished to God that he was my dad because he was a really cool guy. Anyway, after the police left I told my foster parents, "I think I'm ready for some help because I'm starting to fall apart mentally. I'd like to go somewhere."

So they took me to a psycho ward, and I told them that this is what I wanted. I said, "I would like help with this. I want to be the real me. I do not want to be something that somebody tried to create." I was there for about two weeks, and I was no problem. It was weird because I'm sitting around with a bunch of crazy psychos.

It didn't help. My mental problems had started a couple years before that. Between the ages of fourteen and sixteen, I tried to commit suicide about four times. When I tried to commit suicide, I would take pills. I mean a lot of pills, hundreds of them each time.

I also started to have problems with aggressive behaviors. In the locker room when I played football, I whipped up on two or three of my teammates. I head-butted a couple of people on the football field because they would call me n----- this and n----- that. I wouldn't have gave a s--- but one day this dude said, "You n-----, get to the back of the line." I turned around and head-butted him and split open his forehead. The coach asked him what happened, and he wouldn't say anything because he knew the coach wouldn't be happy with what he said. I was called the "n" word a lot, and I'm not even African American.

Critical Thinking Questions

1. **What is your reaction to this obviously abusive story?**

2. **Is such abusive treatment of foster children confined to orphanages and homes in other nations, or is it also found in the United States?**

3. **Are you surprised that this young man did not get into more trouble as an adolescent?**

4. **Why did he try to commit suicide as often as he did?**

5. **What does he need in his life to be more content and adjusted?**

A PERSON OF GREAT PROMISE

People have always come to me for advice. I'll have ex-girlfriends from four or five years ago calling me up and saying, "Such and such and such happened. What should I do?" I would say, "Why should you call me? For one thing, your boyfriend isn't going to like that you're calling me, because you and me used to be together."

I met my father recently after twenty-one years, and after listening to him, I realized that I am from him and can see what other people see in me because I see the same thing in him. My father makes things that totally are not interesting, interesting.

I don't know what I want to do yet. But I want to take it to the top. I want to practice law, I want to be in real estate. I would like to have my own half-hour television show.

It basically starts out that my mom was born in 1955, and my father was born in 1949. So, by the time they were teenagers, they were in the 1970s. He is blacker than black, and she is whiter than white. He was the oldest of thirteen kids. His parents were not around, and he raised his brothers and sisters pretty much by himself.

Obviously, my mom's parents didn't like the fact that she was with a black man. She went against their wishes and moved away with him. They were married, but my dad became abusive.

The first child they had was given up for adoption by my grandparents. There were four kids after that who were aborted. I was the sixth child, and I should not have made it as far as I did. My dad took me under his wing, and he wouldn't let me out of his sight.

I had a little brother after that, and he got favorite treatment. I am not quite sure why. I don't know how receptive my grandparents were to us. We would stay up there when school was out, like in the summertime. We never left the house. We would have to go out to the back yard or downstairs to the basement. When they came down to visit us, we could go out, play ball, or do whatever we wanted.

They're great people, and I love them. I don't hold anything against them. That was how they thought. It was the times, but they have changed. They're not like that anymore. However, my grandfather still shows that he is a little bigoted.

My mother is a tough woman. She raised two bi-racial kids by herself. She went back to school. We were in and out of battered shelters. We were sharing toys with other kids and sleeping on cots. We were living life but just barely living, not really enjoying it.

When I met my father, I learned a lot. He told that their problems started when I was one. My parents sent me down to live with his family in Alabama when I was two. My uncle was probably thirty-two or thirty-four, and he sexually abused me every day for eight months. I don't have an actual memory of the abuse incidents, except for one time. It really screwed up my thinking. It confused me. You just don't know what is right or wrong anymore. As a child, you are not capable of understanding how people view pedophilia.

My uncle was the youngest of thirteen siblings, and he was the first to die. I'm glad the Lord took him before I had a chance to kill him. That is how I feel. When my father met me recently, one of the first things he said to me was, "I thought you would be gay."

I never really understood this whole experience. I never knew what had taken place to me before I got into elementary and then high school and learning all about that stuff. I didn't think your family could do something like that to you.

There was tension between my mom's parents and my father. She went back to him, repeatedly. Even though my grandparents would tell her to stay, she would go back to him. They would tell her, "If you go back, we won't do this and we won't do that for you." She would still go back.

Eventually, we ended up settling in where I now call home. We didn't have the best apartment, a lot of clothes, or TVs, but we had each other. It is like a Greek tragedy.

Sports is what kept me out of trouble. My great love is basketball. I could have gotten a college scholarship in a lower-division program to play basketball. I still daydream, and I'm twenty-four about playing in the NBA. I don't think that dream will ever stop.

When I was six or seven, I began to understand my surroundings. Hey, I don't have a father. Hey, my mom is white and we're black. I wondered whether people on the outside viewed us as confused kids. It was a bad two- or three-year period.

I did get into a lot of fights for the smallest things—a momma joke. My mom had gone through so much s--- that to put her name in your month, you had it coming. Or to call me a n-----, or to steal something from me.

My little brother and I fought other kids a lot. A couple times cops would take us to the station for fighting, but we never had charges filed against us. We were never sent to boot camp or anything like that. I wasn't out looking for a fight, but if my brother was, I was down with him.

My mother had a brain hemorrhage in 1997 or 1998. I was shooting baskets at school. Something told me to go home. I said, "OK, if I make the next two shots, I'll go home. Otherwise, I'll stick around." I made them and went home. I opened the door, and my mother yelled to me, "I can't move my leg. I can't move my leg." She had a vessel bust in her brain and lost control of all her bodily functions. I got her to the doctor, and he told me, "If you would have gotten here two minutes later, she would have died."

Through high school I made good grades and played football, basketball, and baseball. I did some stealing but never got caught. We stole alcohol from the Hy-Vee grocery store. I probably hit Hy-Vee up for two or three thousand dollars one summer. I have assault charges up the ass. I drank a little underage, but not much. I smoked a little weed. I did a little bit more, but not much.

We did really stupid things. I will show you how stupid we were. The apartment building adjacent to us is where we would go to steal things. The next day we would go and do it again. One day this kid called me the "n" word, and my brother and I went to his work and ended up getting into a fight with a customer. This is one of the times that we got taken down to the station, but nothing really happened. The customer must not have pressed charges on us or something.

Growing up, it could have been a lot worse. I was in a really bad neighbourhood, with the projects and all that. We heated our house with our oven; we would cut a pizza up in more than eight pieces so it looked like you had more to eat.

I did have a problem in my college years. I was in a club with my ex-girlfriend. She ended up hitting one of the girls who was coming on to me. The bouncer thought that I had hit the girl. He said something like, "Aren't you guys supposed to be hitting your own girls like that; don't come to the club and hit our girls." He was white and came at me with that racial tone. So, I spit in his face. There were police officers standing around, and I knew if I punched him I would go to jail. I got taken down as if I had a bomb on me. I guess when I was taken down a cop scratched his knee. I got charged with a simple misdemeanor for spitting and an aggravated misdemeanant because the cop had scratched his knee in taking me to the ground. They really put the mace on me. I spent the night in jail, took a plea bargain, and was on probation for two years. I had over $1,000 in fines to pay off. In November of this year, I was taken off formal probation.

I learned from this situation that our public defender's system is horrible. The situation made me want to change the system even more. I will be graduating this May; then I want to go to law school, and I would eventually like to run for office. Then, I should be in a position where I will be able to change the system.

Critical Thinking Questions

1. **This young man has exceptional talent. He is particularly insightful, one of the more insightful young persons one of the coauthors has come across in a long time. How do you think his future will work out?**

2. **How much do you think his trauma and deprivations as a child and adolescent will affect him as an adult?**

3. **Why do you believe that he did, as he puts it, "really stupid things" as an adolescent?**

I NEVER GOT CAUGHT

My father has worked at John Deere for thirty years, and my mother is a guard there. My younger sister is an accountant, and my younger brother is going to school to be a pharmacist.

My home life as a child was not the greatest. My parents would fight, and my father would slap all of us around. He was a diabetic and would have many insulin reactions that would bring this on. So I grew up in a lot of violence.

When I reached middle school, I would spend the weekends at my friend's home who had a sixteen-year-old sister who could drive. She would get us beer. We drank a lot of beer at this time, and I drank out of my first beer bong at the age of thirteen. I did it to get away from my home life and, before I knew it, I was getting drunk every weekend. This continued throughout my high school career.

I also began shoplifting. I would steal cigarettes for my friends and me. It wasn't long before smoking became a habit for me. There was one time when I was almost caught shoplifting thousands of dollars worth of stuff, but I managed to get away without getting caught. It became so easy for me to steal items. I would walk into a store and walk right out with a brand-new winter jacket on me. I did this three times at the same store. I also experimented with marijuana a few times, but I just did it to go along with others. I never really got high from it.

I did run away from home a few times throughout my adolescence. My dad would slap me with a belt and punch me. This finally enraged me enough to run away. I eventually began to fight back when he tried to do these things to me.

I do remember one incident when I was sixteen. I was driving my parents' car drunk down a busy street and ran into a man on a motorcycle. I panicked and drove away. In my hysterical state of consciousness, I turned down another street and almost hit a parked car. Low and behold, I was never caught for this incident.

When I got away with this, it made it easier for me to repeat my drunk driving over and over. I did it many times without getting into any trouble with the law, until one night, when I went to the senior kegger. I was only a junior at the time and went there to get drunk. I decided to leave early and cruise around (still drunk). I was playing around with my radio and crashed into the car in front of me. The cops came and knew I had been drinking, but they did not arrest me. Instead, they called my parents, and my father came to pick me up. On the way home, he threatened to kill me and even started to hit me severely. I kicked him in the face and got out of the car. I ran to a house and called the police to inform them what had happened. My father was arrested.

Throughout high school I had a curfew but rarely followed it. My parents were very strict with me since my older sister got pregnant her senior year in high school. I was not sexually active, but they didn't know that. They took it upon themselves to set strict rules for me. It didn't affect me at all. I would come home whenever I wanted and would sneak out of the house whenever I felt the need to. This caused my dad a lot of distress.

I never got caught shoplifting and was never in trouble with the law. The reason I never got caught is that back then the technology wasn't like it is today. I was also very sneaky about it. To steal make-up, I would act like I was picking one item up and grab like three or four things and slip them up my sleeve. I would make sure that they were underneath my tight bands around my wrist. To steal clothes, I would go into the changing room and take the tags off of clothes. I would then hide them behind the mirror and slip what I was wearing before over the newly stolen clothes.

I can honestly say that I do not know how I got away with drinking and driving so much. I don't know how I got away with hitting that man on the motorcycle. That really shook me up, but I went ahead and kept doing it. Even when I hit the other car when I was drunk, I think the officer felt sorry for me and thought that my parents would punish me enough. In all actuality, I should be dead. Even though I did not get caught, it would have been the best for me to be put into a juvenile detention center.

I always knew that my father would worry that I was gone, and I knew that he would want me to come back home. When I did come back home, he would punish me by grounding me for two or three weeks. He would think that I was going to learn my lesson, but I never did. I think I did it to try and show him that I was going to do it anyway, no matter if he liked it or not. As far as making it out on the streets, I would go to a friend's house or my cousin's house and camp out there for a while. I never ran away and had nowhere to go. I knew that sooner or later my father would find me anyway.

I graduated from high school. Three months after high school, I went into the Army and fulfilled my duty. I have been married three times, twice to my current husband, and I have three kids. It has taken me a long time to get through college with all that has happened to me, but I am currently a junior and plan on graduating next May.

Critical Thinking Questions

1. **Why do you think this young person was so incorrigible at home?**

2. **What particular needs did this young person have that were unmet at home?**

3. **Is she correct in her assumption that a short time in detention would have changed her behavior?**

DOING YOUR OWN TIME

You need to come in here and mind your own business. Take care of yourself, don't worry about anybody else. You will not have any problems. You come in here and do your time. This place isn't anything to me. I just come in here and do my time. When my time is up, I will leave.

But to others–they are scared. Some kids are so scared that they try to kill themselves. Some try to be under staff protection. Ninety-nine percent of whites are scared, scared to death. You probably have one or two whites that will fight. It's just that they don't know anything about the streets.

If you are on the streets today, you have to be part of a gang. If you play the gang right, you are going to win. You play it wrong, you lose. Something is going to happen to you. You have to take care of your own.

When I was little, some people told me that this institution was rough. They would kill you, beat you up, and all this. I used to say I didn't want to go here because I would have to kill somebody. You got a lot of people scared of this place. I heard it was rough. Dangerous. You can't turn your back on anyone. That's what I heard.

When I came up in here, I had to fight about six or seven people. But you got a lot of guys in here scared. I'm talking about plain old scared. People giving up commissary. Food. Trays of food. They never eat in here, they are so scared, you know. People giving away food for other people to take care of them.

They are so scared that they tell others, "Take my food. After you get your food, you get mine." You know what I'm saying? If they approach me, I tell them, "You have your own food; you're not getting mine."

You just have to stand up for your rights. You can't back down for anything. You can't let anybody take anything from you. Not me. I'm going to break their m----- f------ neck; I'm going to do something to them. There isn't anybody going to walk up and take something out of my hand. You have to stick up for yourself. They have to know that if they mess with you, you are going to get them in their sleep or something.

There are some guys who let others just walk by and hit them in the head. They turn their heads. They just let them do anything to them. You can't argue with them; that's a waste of time. If you want to protect yourself, make your move, but when you make it, make it right. I'm telling you point-blank.

I have never been around a sexual punk in this institution. Not in my group. You aren't going to find too many fags in our group because we are the aggressive cottage. They have never approached me in no fag way. A punk, to me, is a person who lets everyone walk all over them, including sexually. They don't try to stick up for themselves.

They have a lot of rules in here. Do not disrespect staff. No sexual gestures. No cussing. No talking in the hallway. Pull your pants up, tuck your shirt in when you are walking to school. No fighting. No smoking. Basic rules. People do it anyway. Rules do not matter. Someone is always going to break the rules.

You got two or three staff around here who think they are hard. A couple of staff here tell you to shut the f--- up. Couple of hard staff might say, "Shut the f--- up or I'll throw your ass in lock-up" or, "Set your punk-ass down. You are nothing but a punk." They want to beat somebody. You might be staff, but you must give me some respect if you want some respect in return. You got a couple of them who come across in this way, got a little size on them, and want to push us around.

We do not run this place; staff run it. If we ran it, people would be leaving off grounds, leaving when they wanted to. If I ran this place, I would have some keys in my pocket.

Staff don't care. They don't care about anything but themselves and their paycheck. Some staff come in here, talk that street s---, just like we do. Some of them don't care what you do. Some of them let you walk in the hallway, and some of them come in with buzz s---, like, "This is my m----- f------ cottage. It is going to be run the way I want it to be ran." There isn't really any positive staff here, not to me. The social worker, he will try to help you if he can, but he usually can't do a lot.

You can gamble for anything here. I'm telling you that you can end up owing "lifetime" until you leave or until they leave. If they leave and their tight dude is still here, you have to pay him until you leave. His tight dude is his friend, like a brother. Lifetime means everything you get. You get a tray of food, it is his.

I used to know this one dude. He used to let everybody punk him, everybody bully on him. One day he just woke up. "F--- that, man," he said. "I am through being everybody's punk." He pulled out a mop handle and just started swinging at them. He caught this one dude in the back of the head. Nobody messes with him any more. He just woke up. Now they say he is crazy.

The ones that are on the top are from the streets. The soft ones are the ones who lived in the nice neighborhoods. They just went out one night and got into trouble and came home and told their mothers. They ended up here and don't know what to do.

The one's you have on top, you know, are hoods, like gang members and dope dealers. They know how to play the game, but if you don't have any gang on the street, you have no gang in the joint. If you are from Columbus and you get in a fight, everybody from Columbus is going to help you.

There are a number of ways to bring dope into the institution. Some of them take a bag of reefer and swallow it and go use the bathroom. You have some of them that get staff to bring reefers and other dope in. Then you have some that just know how to get it through. You have some that hide it in their mouth, or they tape it to parts of their body. They might have a little rip in their shoe. While they are being searched, some of them hand it to another person. You go right back and get your clothes on, and the other person hands it right back to you.

Critical Thinking Questions

1. **What is the most difficult problem with being in this training school?**

2. **Why, according to this interviewee, are most of the victims white?**

3. **How much support does this resident feel from staff?**

4. **How accurate do you think the perceptions of this resident are?**

5. **What do you think of the quality of life is in this training school?**

JUVENILE HOMICIDE OFFENDER AND ADJUSTMENT TO A TRAINING SCHOOL

I'm in a juvenile penitentiary. I would explain that the people in here are no different than the people out there, as far as age or mentality, or what they're doing. Take the example you drink, you party, you go around having fun and raising Cain, and so do the guys in here. Except they just got a little too wild, and they got caught. And that's what they're here for. You can go to a certain extent, just don't pass that extent, or you will be here also.

I've been incarcerated for almost five years. I was in another training school before I came here. The other training school was more structured for younger people, age eleven to sixteen. Staff emphasized more on respect for elders, right and wrong. Their school is set up for people of that age group between sixth and ninth grade. You can graduate there; they had the power to do so, but they'd rather you have a vocational trade. That's the reason why I was sent here when I was seventeen. I spent two years there, and I've been here two and a half.

At the other training school, they were a lot more immature and younger. And the guys here are a little more violent than the ones there, because these guys have more aggression naturally than the younger guys do.

The rumors that surround any institution are that it is supposed to be bad; you know about where all the bad guys go, or where all the real hard core criminals go. Guys our age that are hardcore go here. When I finally did get here, you know, I wasn't intimidated by the fact because I knew people who had been here, and they told me what it was like before I ended up here. But at first, I heard that it was really bad; once I got here it wasn't as bad as everybody said. Bad, but not that bad.

The mentality of the students is what bothers me about this place. A lot of the students had the opportunity to come in, had the opportunity to learn; they also had the opportunity to better themselves. But they also had the opportunity to make everything worse on themselves. The staff here do not emphasize an education enough; they do not emphasize what's going on in the student's life, how the student can better himself. Students come in with one mentality; they leave with the same mentality.

I used to drive around, I used to have all the girls liking me, and I used to use drugs. I see people who I knew out there in here, and it's like a family reunion, a hideaway, a party, or a vacation. You go back out there with the same mentality, only you're worse because you know better ways to commit crime. You've experienced new things from being locked up; you have learned new things from talking to other people who've been caught. You find better ways to do what you've done before. The staff don't make you go to school or show you that schooling is important. They're more concerned with keeping you controlled and keeping your aggression on tap.

When you first come in, what they've heard about you will determine how you are dealt with. Myself, I don't even put attention to people who come and go. I've seen so many people

come and go. But students who come in, especially young guys in for homicide, like me, they're supposed to be bad. A lot of people will try them to find out how bad he is.
They will walk up to him and punch him to see what he'll do. Most of the time he won't do nothing for his first year; he won't say nothing or do nothing because he's scared. First time being locked up and he's in here for homicide, and he's scared about getting more time. Sometimes, they push him too far; he reacts and gets extremely violent.

Whites are discriminated against in this institution because the black kids don't like the white kids. They don't get along.

I'm in for homicide. I am six-foot tall and weigh 180 pounds. I can carry my own weight, so I'm not messed with. But a younger guy, say fifteen or sixteen years old, that is real scrawny and comes in for truancy or aggravated burglary can be in real trouble. If the black kids don't like him because he's white and can't carry his own weight, they'll mess with him.

Three guys in our cottage who were white and real small came in. One guy who was black didn't like their attitude and wanted to intimidate them into doing what he wanted them to do. He said, "Hold my cigarettes for me. If I get in trouble for anything I'm doing and get caught, it's you not me." He wanted to intimidate them, so he punched all three of them. That's pretty much the way it goes around here. The smaller guy gets intimidated into doing the dirty work for the more aggressive.

Well, if I wanted someone to do my dirty work, I'd have picked a smaller guy. I'd tell him,"You know you're my boy; don't worry about nobody messing with you." As long as he's by my side, nobody's going to mess with him because he's my boy. Students know not to mess with my boy because you are messing with me, and I will need to deal with it. So they will leave him alone. As long as he is left alone, then he'd do just about anything negative I wanted him to do. If I got cigarettes or some kind of illegal substance, I'd hand it to him and tell him to hold it. If I sold, I'd sell through him. If I sold this man a cigarette, I'd tell him, get it off him.   That's the way you do business. When it came down to a cottage search or a crackdown, they'd bust him with it. He wouldn't rat on me; I wouldn't get in trouble. It keeps me clean.

These fences hold you physically inside, but not mentally. This is an institution. It doesn't mean that you can't get things done outside the fences. Anything I want done, I can get done. I just ask. I'll pay somebody in here who knows somebody personally out there who can get a job done. This guy is always talking about his car. It is real cool. He shows me a picture of it. I get real cool with the guy. "Real nice car; where is it parked?" "Oh, it's in your garage at your house." "What's your address? Tell me your address." Hey, there are guys out there, who just for fun, will go and total this guy's car with ball bats. They will send me a picture, so I'll be in total control of this guy. I could have things done to anybody, anybody.

Don't get me wrong. Those are some of the things that could happen. It doesn't necessarily mean that they go on every day. I'm sure you hear stories about prison. Every day there's a fight, every day somebody gets raped, everyday somebody gets beat up. Somebody goes to the hole for six months. Somebody tries to go AWOL. I mean, these things happen in a prison, and they take place in here also. You don't really hear much about it. It doesn't mean anything to the people who are not involved; it doesn't mean a thing. They don't even care. As far as whether it enhances physical abuse or whatever, I don't think so. To some people, some guys come in here, and they are just play toys to other people. It depends on the individual.

The sexual stuff does go on, but nobody knows who is doing it. We hear stories like, "That guy is a punk, a homosexual; he does sexual favors for cigarettes." If you ask the guy straight out, "Hey man, are you a punk?", he will answer you, "No, I'm not a punk," and he's ready to fight, but deep down inside he knows he's a punk.

I know of an incident where one guy told another, "I'll sell you half a cigarette; what are you going to give me?" He says, "I don't have nothing to give you." The guy says, "I know what you can give me." He says, "What?" "A sexual favor." So he does the sexual favor for the guy, and then the guy helped him smoke the cigarette. He wanted a cigarette so bad, he done a sexual favor for the guy, and then the guy who he bought it from helped him smoke it. Half a cigarette is only about how much? It's like somebody crushed half a cigarette out in the ashtray.

The time I've been here, there have been several sexual incidents. There was the one I just talked about. Another time two guys got together, but they were homosexuals. I remember one rape. Up at Auburn, one guy was assaulted by two other guys. Another guy was involved in it, but all he did was watch.

The rules are fair, but some of the staff aren't fair about the rules. We have a staff on our cottage, I ain't going to mention any names, but he's a real pain. He'll tell you that you're not allowed to do this, you're not allowed to do that. So you take the twenty rules in our cottage, and you write these rules down. Once you've written these rules down, you memorize those rules. He'll walk up to you periodically and ask you any rule right out of the blue. If you can't recite that rule to him, you will write that rule one hundred times. If you don't get that one hundred times done within one hour, you will write it five hundred times. This guy is just a real pain. What he is trying to do is to intimidate us and gain respect that way. He doesn't want to show us respect because he feels that he is better than us. I've studied a lot of psychology. This guy thinks he deserves respect because he is over top of us.

He carries the keys to the doors. He can lock you up anytime he wants; there's nothing you can do about it, nothing. He can lock you in your room for two or three days because of an incident that is so petty that other staff wouldn't even look at it. They wouldn't even think twice about it. People hate him. He knows people hate him, but he keeps going at it. He's pushing people. He's been involved with three fights with youth in the institution since he's been here.

There's a law among the students here: you see no evil, hear no evil, speak no evil, and your ass stays out of hot water. If I hit a guy, you didn't see a thing even though you are standing there watching me. You didn't see a thing. Snitches get stitches is the big thing they say around here.

There's a guy on our cottage who owed out "lifetime," and staff told him not to pay. And he said, "Alright," and he didn't pay. The guy came up and beat him up for not paying, and said, "You better start paying me again, or you're going to get it again." Well, he went and told the staff, so he got beat up twice as bad. Then somebody that wasn't his business, somebody done something, and he went and told the staff. He got beat up real bad then, and staff put him into another cottage. They told him, "You know, we're going to send you to a different cottage; you're getting beat up too much down here." They sent him to another cottage, and he got right back into the same situation. So they sent him to another, and he's been in three cottages since. Every time he goes to a different cottage he gets into the same predicament.

There are students here who have more control than the staff do. There are students here that the staff sort of loan their control to. If a student is an intimidator, manipulates power over the other students, and the staff feels they have no control over that student, they'll give that student leeway to do as he pleases. So, he can tell everybody what to do, when to do it, and why. Some of the students here are aggressive and don't have respect for anyone, but you better give them respect or else. I guess you can call them bullies. They'll tell you when you're going to do something and offer no explanation at all. The staff enjoy this because they can sit back and collect easy money.

Because I have four-and-a-half years under my belt, nobody can get over me. Everybody in the institution looks at me as either half crazy for being able to do the time or extremely aggressive. I'm not aggressive, and I'm not crazy. I get along with everybody. So I get a lot of respect just because of my time. I'm white. Black kids get the most respect in here because there are more of them than there are whites, and most of the whites are small skinny guys. I don't buddy with nobody, so I can't be a follower, but I guess I'm more of an individual than a leader.

In here there are three different types. There are your followers, your leaders, and your individuals, and I put myself on top, as an individual. You'd have your individuals on the top rung, cause they don't bother nobody, nobody bothers them. They do their time; most of them learn while they're here, and staff like them because they don't cause any problems. They don't mess with the other students. They don't mess with staff, and staff don't mess with them. Everything goes fine with them. Your intimidators or leaders are staff's eyes and ears. They can do whatever they want; staff won't really say much. None of the students will contradict anything that they do. They have their control, as far as the group goes. Students that are followers are the punks and people who want to be cool with the leaders. So, when leaders see something on TV and laugh, everybody else laughs, especially the followers.

Critical Thinking Questions

1. **How does this resident's perception of training school differ from that of the resident in the previous story? How would you describe the staff in this facility?**

2. **According to this resident, does the seriousness of your offense in the community make a difference in how a youth is accepted in the peer culture?**

3. **Do you believe that this resident is accurate that aggressive peers are able to intimidate and control staff? If you were the superintendent of a training school in which this was taking place, how would you deal with it?**

4. Does this resident believe that training schools are good? Does he believe that the influence of training school makes a youth more or less criminogenic? Be specific.

5. What can be done to make training schools more humane and constructive for those placed within them?

I HAVE BEEN AROUND, YOU KNOW

I am the youngest of five. I got two brothers and two sisters. My mom raised us all, and we were all together. My dad lived with us until I was six years old. When he was with us, it was all good. He worked at John Deere and made good money. We had a big house, and life was good. It was good up until my mom started smoking crack. She spent all the money and kicked my dad out.

After my dad left, my mom worked two jobs, and we were poor. Throughout my childhood, I would sell drugs.

One Christmas, when I was seven, I got a BB gun. I thought I was so cool. I was running around the neighborhood with it one day, and my friends dared me to shoot the bus with it. I pumped it up a few times and hid on the porch to wait for the bus. The bus came up, and I shot it. I remember the window shattering; I ran upstairs, threw my BB gun in my closet, and ran to school a block away. So, I am sitting in class. During this time, the police called my mom home from work, and she showed the police my BB gun. She immediately called the school to have me come home. When I got there, the police asked me if I shot the bus window out. I told them it was an accident. They took me down to the police station at seven years old. When I got home, my momma whooped me and took my gun away from me. This was the first time I got into trouble with the law.

The next year was really rough. My dad was gone, and our family didn't have much money. My mom would give us each $100 at the beginning of the school year for clothes and shoes, and then halfway through the school year she would give us another $100 for clothes. This was our Christmas present. One time, when I was about eight years old, my friend and I caught the city bus from the east side of town and took the bus (with no supervision at all) to the mall. When we were at the mall, we would go to the game stores and test out the new games and look for stuff to steal. When we were in Sears, I found a couple things, and I took off with them. My friend took longer and got busted on camera. I was outside and ditched the things I stole, and went back inside to find my friend. When I found him, he was walking with the police. They saw me and grabbed me too. I denied everything, but they showed me the surveillance tape, and I knew that I was busted. They cuffed me, called my mom, and she came and got me. When we got home, she whooped me up good, and put me on punishment. My punishment wasn't bad at all because my mom worked two jobs. So when I got home from school, I stayed inside until my mom went to work at KFC [Kentucky Fried Chicken]. Then I was alone until ten at night. I could roam around the neighborhood all I wanted.

This is when things started to get real bad. At around nine or ten years old, I realized that I was poor and that I needed some stuff. I had no supervision over me at all. My older brother was into track and sports. I always thought that he was going to grow up to be famous, but it all ended his senior year when he dropped out of school. My middle brother wasn't into school at all. He was, and still is, a gangster, a Crip. I was really close to my middle brother. We shared the same bunk bed. When I was ten years old, my brother would go to his gang meetings every Sunday. I remember one time when he came home with a black eye. I asked him what happened, and he told me that he got it while playing football. But I knew that he never played football. So I kept harassing him, and he told me he got beat into the Crips.

After this, he was sporting his colors and hanging out with my cousin, dealing drugs in his Cadillac. This made me tell myself that I wanted to be a Crip. All of the people that I was hanging out with were in gangs. Some were GDs [Gangster Disciples], and some were Crips. The GDs and the Crips didn't mess with each other much. They could work together.

We moved out of the neighborhood when I was ten. My mom still worked two jobs, and I never saw her much. I knew she loved me and cared for me, but she wasn't around much. At this time, my cousin was an OG [Original Gangster], and him and his friend would go get drugs out of state, and bring them back to our town and sell them for profit. They always came to my house. My oldest brother, at this time, also got beat into the Crips. I was thinking, "This is it. I am going to go to a meeting and get beat in!" So I went to the next meeting, and they wouldn't let me in. They said I was too young. I hadn't even hit puberty yet. They still hung out with me and let me ride with them. I was watching them sell drugs, and they were feeding me.

When I turned twelve, my cousin (who was a 111 Crip) took me under his wing. We were celebrating my birthday, having a barbeque, and all of a sudden these two kids (fourteen to fifteen years old) jumped on me and started kicking my ass for about a minute. They finally took them off me and told me I was a Crip. I was twelve years old and a Crip. They told me that I could work my way up pretty easy. So, here I was, twelve years old and selling drugs on the street and smoking weed. I bought my first car when I was twelve years old.

When I was thirteen years old, I was on the street corner selling drugs one day. I never knew that I was being videotaped by the police. After a while, when they came up, I ran away and ditched my drugs. They ended up catching this fat dude, and he told them that the drugs were mine. The next day the cops were at my house with a warrant for possession of crack cocaine. They sent me to the detention center for three months. They let me out on house arrest in December until I went to trial, because I said that the drugs were not mine. I had my mom's word going for me because they showed her the videotape, and I was wearing my Starter jacket (which she didn't know I had bought). She told them that it couldn't be me on the video because I didn't have that jacket.

The officer, on the other hand, said he knew it was me, and they found me guilty of possession with the intent to deliver. I went back to a residential program and stayed there for five months. I was being good and programming, but I got frustrated when I would see people come in and out and I was still there. Everyone else was cussing, so one day I came in all cussing and stuff, and they placed me in another part of the residential program for violating my parole. This was for a couple of weeks, and then they sent me to the state's training school.

I was there for six months and breezed through the program. I didn't get into any trouble. They sent me back to the residential program, and I attended the high school in my part of town. They wouldn't let me go back to my family. They told me that I needed to complete their program first. Eight months later, they just kicked me out of it without graduating. They told me that I had gained the maximum benefits from it. I didn't care at the time. I just wanted to go back home.

I'm not going to say that I lost ties with my mother over this time, but it's hard to get back into things after something like this. My mom moved into a four-bedroom house, and my sister had a baby while I was gone. So there were seven people living in this tiny-ass house, but we made it work. This let me get back into the streets with my brother for about three months. During this time, he caught another drug charge and got sent to prison because he was eighteen. Before he left, he gave me some drugs to sell. I was back on the streets, but I still went to class and got good grades. At the same time, I was selling weed and crack.

One day I was on the streets, and I got out of my car to fight this dude. He was mad because I was flirting with his girlfriend. He ended up calling the cops, and I got busted. I got sent back to the training school. All they caught me with was the drugs that I had in my jacket (which was weed), because I swallowed the drugs that were in my mouth. I breezed through the program again. I was there a total of five months. I made Honor Corps and everything because I knew how to work the system. The head man told me that they had never seen anybody go through the program like I did. He also told me that he didn't want me to go, but he said that I was so goal-oriented and could see that I wanted to achieve something in my life.

He ended the conversation by telling me that they were not going to take me back if I got into trouble again. This was it. If I got into trouble again, I was looking to go somewhere else. This was OK for me, because I wasn't planning on getting into more trouble.

After I met with the head man, I met with my counselor. He told me that he had a deal for me that I couldn't refuse. He told me I could graduate from the high school at the training school, and he had a scholarship for me to attend a local community college. I told him, "No, I want to go back to the high school near where I lived and graduate from there." After that, he told me that I was stupid and that I was going to go back and f--- up. I said, "Whatever, man!"

I returned home and went back to the streets selling drugs. By this time, we had declared our own gang–the East Side Logan Avenue Crips. All this time we had been claiming that we were 30's Crip and 111 Crips when none of us had ever been to Colorado. So we made our own gang. All we did was sit on Logan Ave and sell drugs all day long from a crack house. We were making good money. I was the key supplier of the crack house. I can honestly say that I have handled around $1 million. I have many pairs of shoes, clothes, and a few cars that aren't cheap. I was *deep* in the gang.

Let me tell you how I ended up in prison. My brother stashed his drugs at my mom's house. I had my own house, but my brother stashed his drugs at mom's. Somebody found out and broke into the house when my mom was not home. They took everything. It was about $30,000 worth. So he was broke and losing his mind. He wanted to do something about it. Our town is small, and there were many rumors flying around about who did it.

So one day we were in my 1994 Suburban (my brothers, my OG cousin, and another cousin who was staying with us for the summer), and we were driving around. We were going to find out who took the drugs. I had two felons with me, and we were driving around. We had heard that Timmy was the one who broke into the house. We saw him at the park. My brother got out of the car and said, "I'm going to get this dude!" My brother confronted him about the drugs, and he denied everything. He said it was all crazy s---. He wanted to talk to who told us that it was him.

He got into my Suburban willingly. We were all talking s--- to him but never once touched him. We drove off. By this time, Timmy's friends called the police and told them that we had kidnapped their friend, even though he got into the car on his own. We were driving around looking for this dude who told us it was Timmy, and sure enough the police pulled us over with their guns drawn. They asked Timmy to get out of the car, and he was saying, "Help me. They are going to kill me!" He said we had guns and all of this s---. So they took us down to the police station and questioned all of us separately. I kept quiet and didn't say a word because I knew they didn't have a case on us.

My brother ended up telling what had happened, and they charged us with third-degree kidnapping. We all bonded out except for my cousin, the OG. They had a no-bond for him, and he was facing a big charge. We all pled to lesser charges with the prosecutor, but when it came time for the judge to sentence us, he pretty much said that there is no way we could have the deals. So, we all went to prison. I was sentenced to two years in prison and served ten months.

I got out, am staying away from selling drugs, and am now in college. My girlfriend just had a baby. I never want to go back to prison.

Critical Thinking Questions

1. **Is it surprising that this individual would get into selling drugs the way he did?**

2. **What role did gangs play in his life?**

3. **Why was this individual able to do so well in institutions and yet experience so many problems adjusting to community life?**

A LONGING FOR STREET SUPERIORITY

I have always believed that if I displayed hard work, motivation, and, most of all, perseverance, I could have the life I aimed for. What I aimed for, dreamed of, was a lavish three-story loft in the downtown area overseeing San Francisco, tailor-made clothes, horses, a nice boat or two, jewels, and, of course, women.

I have believed that what separated me from the rest was my having heart. I was ready for whatever. My code of ethics required that I first must have a plan. Second, I would prepare for action. Third, I would execute these actions, and, fourth, I would make sure that nobody f---- - up my operation or else they would die, point blank.

Personally, I was never the bully type when I was young. I just had a hunger to get money and was always taught not to let anybody f---- me over.

My mom worked second shift for years. After work, she would go straight to the local hole in the wall of a bar and drink her stressful day away. So most of the time I only saw her for about the amount of time it takes to pass a partially closed door on my way to school. Inside the door was her room, where she slept the morning away, not concerned if I was going to school or not. And yes, I went to school regularly.

I went to school mostly because I knew they served breakfast and lunch. But at night I wasn't so lucky. I would get awakened by the slam of doors followed by my mother pounding bags of White Castle burgers on the table, yelling to my sister and me, to quote her, "Come get this g-- d--- food before it gets cold. And if you don't eat it all, I'm going to kick your ass for making me wait in line and wasting my g-- d--- money."

If we didn't eat all the food, she held true to her word. See, at an early age, I knew that money was the factor, and I was going to have to get it myself. I couldn't rely on my mother to do s--- for me except let me live under her roof, p--- in her toilet, and use her pots and pans if I somehow had something to cook.

At times, I look back when I had to go to school with the same s--- on that I had the day before and sometimes three days in a row. I mean, it was bad. I find it hard to remember when my mother actually bought me clothes from the store. I came from a large family—five aunts, six uncles, and a city full of cousins. So hand-me-downs was something that my family had practiced for years.

I was just starting high school. I knew my classmates would laugh at me because of my clothes. I couldn't get my mom to buy me a damn thing. I also had been moved up to the varsity football team, so even more people knew who I was. I was being noticed. I knew that I had to do something. I wanted to look good when I hung out with the upper classmen. I wasn't about to watch those dudes walk around with all the girls, nice cars, fresh clothes, and jewelry. I wanted this for myself.

But it was a tough time for me to shine because my sister had left San Francisco and enlisted in the Navy. My older cousin, Chino, who was like my big brother, was doing time for an armed robbery. So there was no support for anything that I was trying to do. When my sister started making that government money, she would send me $100–$200 a month.

This is when I came up with my first plan. I would save for two months and would go shopping for new clothes, all in the effort to fit in with the in-crowd. In the process of saving my money, my skills and eagerness on the football field started to show even more. In the first two games, I rushed for 413 yards and scored four touchdowns, all over 35 yards.

We were ranked first in the state, I'm the starting running back, and I was getting more attention due to the fact that I was the rookie from the hood. I was destined to be a star. I worked to be the best at what I did, and I was quickly surrounded by those who were making big money from drugs.

Have you ever seen how a fifteen-year-old boy from the bottomless pit who has never had s--- but hand-me-downs and White Castles acts when he sees a wad of money being handed to him? Well, imagine how I acted when I got two stacks in one week, just for running circles around linebackers and safeties and showing my face around town with these big timers.

Since I really didn't have any guidance from home, the streets showed me the direction I should walk in. I mean, at first I wasn't deep into anything like drugs because sports were my first priority. I was playing ball, doing the same thing that everybody else was doing, but I got benefits for doing it.

Through years and years of friends, there was one that always stuck out like a sore thumb. His name was Rico. This dude and me had everything in common, from the favorite college and pro teams, to taste in women.

Rico and I were like a two-man gang. Nothing could come between us. Wherever he would go, I would go. If I got in trouble, nine times out of ten it was because of him. If he got into trouble, nine times out of ten it was because of me.

When he entered high school, his situation was just like mine. He didn't have much support from home. All he relied on was his athletic ability. Like me, he was quickly moved up to varsity. This was my friend; he felt my pain, and I felt his.

When I started getting all the attention and money from the big timers, Rico was going to be the first person in line to make some real money with me. He had a lot of knowledge about drug sales because his cousin was a small timer in the JVL projects, one of the most cutthroat projects in the United States.

I remember one time I had a conversation with Rico's cousin, who said, "I live every day like it's my last one, and then one day it will be." But at the same time, he believed in building up the 'hood'. I mean, if a bag of anything gets sold anywhere, he was using the profits to get something done in the neighborhood.

One time a crack head was killed because he broke into an old lady's house and stole her air conditioner in order to swap it for some drugs. It was OK to swap for the drugs, but it wasn't OK to steal it from an eighty-seven-year-old lady in the middle of July when it was ninety-six degrees.

After practice, Rico and I would go to the JVL projects. It was fun as hell. I mean we lived a carefree life there. We had money and women, power and unlimited weed to smoke there. We were 'hood' stars. We had no worries. We had all of the name brand clothes and nice chains. We weren't old enough to drive yet, but we had a car or two to show off.

At the end of the football season, we had more time to hang out. We had stopped playing the other sports because they weren't as fun as they used to be. At the time I didn't know that I was falling deeper and deeper into the street game.

After I began to get known around town, the big-timer started to let me tap along when he handled major business. I was learn how to communicate with other dealers in hopes that one day I could make a major transaction by myself. Most of the dealers were cool. They talked about how well I had done the previous season and how they couldn't wait to see me play ball again the next year. I was comfortable. Everything seemed to be easy.

I was a natural. I had a way of making people feel comfortable and relaxed. I knew without a doubt I could do it on my own. I had saved enough money to purchase the minimal amount of weed I could from one of the big-timers. I knew that dealing with the white girl, better known as coke, things wouldn't have been so smooth and easy. I saw a lot of people get screwed over with that stuff.

But weed was a piece of cake, so I started buying from the big-timer. You can see how my mental state had changed within a year. First, I was saving money for clothes to fit in. Now I was going to sell because I knew I would be good at it. I had the connections from dealing with the big-timers. I also had the market to sell it. I had classmates, friends, teammates, and even teachers and coaches who I knew would be smoking weed.

I tended to keep business and family separate because that never mixes. When I started off, I immediately made Rico my right-hand man. I could trust him. I knew I wouldn't have to worry about his lying or doing business on the side.

To get things jump started, Rico's cousin fronted us about six guns and two bulletproof vests. Then, we promised on each other's lives two things: if we got caught we would not talk, and we would kill whoever tried to f--- us over. Keep in mind that we were only entering our second year of high school, and we had that kind of mentality.

I mean why not—we could pull it off, right? Age didn't matter on the streets. It was then and still is about the survival of the fittest. We were ready. We had guns and crews with guns. It was about time for us to start football practice again, but this time Rico wasn't playing because he made all D's and F's. This gave us more time to make sure the operation was going to go as smooth as it needed to.

Rico and me decided to make it a joint partnership to ensure that neither one of us got too big for the other. It was something like a check-and-balance thing. We knew we would have to make sure our workers got paid. For some, money was the payoff; for others, the drugs would have been enough. And believe it or not, the girls got a rush off of being involved, so they weren't even looking for pay. We still kept them looking nice, with the best clothes and hairstyles. We wanted to make Rico's cousin a part of the management; he would make the same amount of money as Rico and me. We knew that if he wasn't satisfied, he had the muscle to cause conflict.

I know that it may sound a bit too much for a high school kid to handle, but I was in the middle of everything. I made things happen for everybody, and everybody knew that I had the smarts to run a real operation.

After about six months strong into the game, we began to get more and more advanced in what we did. The operation was so strong that no one had a complaint. It seemed like we were on top after only being in the business for a short amount of time. I knew that there would be controversy ahead, but I had faith that Rico and me would persevere.

Before I knew it, the first problem occurred. The big-timer who taught me the ropes was brutally murdered. In the street and drug game, anything goes. I was suspected to have a hand in that. Not only were they wrong, they were stupid.

At that point, I was starting a life that many don't get a chance to get out of. But I didn't care. I was the man with no record, and I had the weed game in the palm of my hands. After a few more months, I was a year into the game. Rico had completely quit school because he thought he had made enough money that he didn't need an education.

Here I was a junior in high school with great potential to go to college and play ball. But there I was selling weed, all because I wanted to fit in and be a part of the in crowd. I had become popular, on the football field, in school, and on the streets.

And even if I did want to get out, I couldn't because too many people depended on me. I felt like a lost soul. If you have ever had that feeling, then you understand what I'm talking about. When I was younger, I went to church every Sunday with my grandfather, who was the pastor. There I was taught how to live a righteous life. But in my time of turmoil, I refused to look for guidance from my spiritual leader. I knew I was sinning, and I still didn't care.

I mean, I really felt like a person who had committed every sin there is, except for suicide. What did I have to live a righteous life for now? I really felt like I had sold my soul to the devil for the cheap price of fame. I explained to Rico that I had come to the point of no return. I had seen murders take place.

I decided to get out of it. Rico and his cousin took over the operation. Rico was shot but survived. They have done some jail and prison time, but will probably deal drugs the rest of their lives.

I went to college in the Midwest on a football scholarship. Everything was sweet, and then I blew out my knee. College has been all right. My grades are not the greatest, but I only have another semester before graduation. I have a daughter and am trying to work things out with my child's mother.

My roommate and I have sold some weed in college. Then, we decided last summer to sell some ecstasy pills. I had them sent to me through the mail. Somehow, law enforcement learned of it and came and arrested us. I was lucky the feds did not pick the case up. I pled guilty because the county attorney assured me that I would get only a suspended sentence. I would have to serve five years probation, and my fines would be waved. In April of 2006, I appeared for my sentencing hearing, and the judge granted me a deferred sentence. This means that once I have served my probation, the charge will be removed from my record. The county attorney was furious and stormed out of the courtroom.

My sister is now out of the Navy, and she comes to see me at least once a month. As for my mom, I know it may sound cheesy, but I'm glad that she put me through what she did because it made me a stronger person. I now value everything I work for because there was a time when I didn't have a lot of the things I wanted.

After college, I want to work with troubled youth, so I can prevent them from making the same mistakes I did. I want to show them that everyone doesn't get lucky enough to get out of the drug game alive. I survived my high school experiences and more recent experiences, and I will never go that way again.

Critical Thinking Questions

1. **What factors in this young man's life led him to become involved in dealing drugs?**

2. **Is it surprising that he will be graduating from college in the near future?**

3. **Why do you think the judge gave him a deferred sentence?**

4. **If you were his teacher, would you have gone to court on his behalf for the sentencing hearing?**

IT WAS THE RUSH!

Well, actually, I'm just coming to this conclusion as a result of my counseling here that my problems started at birth. I had problems sleeping and was up at night a lot. I always wanted to be eating, wanting to be doing something, you know, have a feeling other than what I was feeling. In thinking back, my mom said that as a baby I needed a lot of attention, a lot of stimulation. I guess I was never just OK with being content and playing by myself, and things that some other kids do at a really early age.

I think it's genetic, because it doesn't affect my brothers and sisters, and we're all pretty close in age. I think there is something organically or biologically different in my brain that I've had since I was really young. I had trouble getting along with other kids from the age of kindergarten. I was disruptive, I couldn't sit still, and they didn't have a name for it forty years ago. Hyperactivity—teachers didn't know what it was. I was bored very easily. I can remember my dad taking us to a parade when I was five. I didn't know what the big deal was. The only part I liked was when they threw the candy out, and I wanted to go home after that.

I would just find more ways and means to stimulate myself. I started shoplifting at an early age. I would go down to a big department store down the street from our house and steal jewelry and cigarettes, anything that could give me a thrill. I remember being nine or ten and my mom taking us to piano lessons on the north side of Pittsburgh. I would walk across a nearby bridge just to look around, just to see and watch people. I'd watch the street activity over in the red light district. It amused me, it excited me, it got me going.

I don't think I really realized at that point it was anything. I knew that I was different, and I was told there was something wrong, but I didn't have a sense of what it was. And then I got into drugs at the age of twelve, and I started smoking pot. It kind of relaxed me, and it put me in with a different group of people. It got me some acceptance with some other people at school.

Some, but not all of them, had the same problems and to the same degree that I did. I can remember being the leader of the pack. Others of them would be like, "Oh well, I wouldn't think about doing that." But me, I was like, "Well, c'mon." I don't think some of them were as far along as I was.

I went from marijuana to cocaine and diet pills, anything that could speed me up. I can remember the diet pills giving me a sense of well-being and accomplishment. They actually made me feel real slowed down. They give me an opposite effect. Made me feel a little more focused.

Then, I just got into a lot of trouble at school, a lot of problems, a lot of turmoil all of the time. Well, I wouldn't say the police knew who I was at that point, but I certainly put my parents through a lot of stuff. It wasn't easy for them. I was grounded a lot of the time, and my parents put a deadbolt on my bedroom door that only locked from the outside. They had to look into private schools and send me somewhere because nobody wanted me in school. Maybe I had an addiction to the drama of it all.

I dropped out of college, I lost a lot of jobs, and I got married. My husband had a lot of drugs, and I liked his drugs. He was a high-rolling dealer, had a fancy lifestyle, and he had this big house in the North Hills. I liked the lifestyle. We would go to Heaven (a nightclub) at night with his friends and do a lot of night clubbing. And I liked that lifestyle and was very addicted to that lifestyle, the excitement. The marriage had its own problems in the things you have to deal with, the places you have to go, drug addiction, and degradation. A lot of stuff in the marriage was homosexual and bisexual with both of us; things that were not nice happened. Kind of in the background, I remember my boyfriend robbing a grocery store and bringing home $16,000 one time. I was just waiting for him to get home. The money lasted a week.

I'm actually just becoming aware of a lot of stuff right now. We have talked about stimulation and, even in my first recovery ten years ago, I never looked at things as stimulation. I was out charging up things all the time, running up my credit card bills, and always looking for something to fill me up.

Part of the reason my life has changed is because of my therapist. I ended up getting clean at twenty-five, finding the program and getting into NA at twenty-five years old. Now, I think having a woman therapist who has been through a lot of stuff and knows what she's talking about has really helped. And I'm able to listen, and I'm ready to listen. I just don't want to be on that same road again. I want to have a happier choice of a life.

We were laughing last night at the church that something had happened with somebody called Maggie in the program, and on the way home I saw Maggie, and she was talking to the people at the church. I said, "Maggie, I have to tell you what happened." And the lady at the church said, "Oh you guys love the drama, don't you?" I can't just wait until I get home and talk to you about it later. No, "Check this out—now!"

So, yeah, I get a high off that energy. I like a high, still today. That's why I walk, talk, and do some things I do. I like the feeling. I like the endorphins going. But it's very hard, and I have to stay focused. And the only way I get focused is if I get the endorphins going for me so that I can come back and be settled and focused on what I'm doing. So once I get up on that excitement high I need to focus to get it under control. And I think just getting enough help to stay focused—and it's scary to think actually about leaving here—and living an old life clean even for me is scary. My life—even clean—was terrible. When I look back, it wasn't terrible, but it wasn't a nice, good, solid, peaceful life.

To stay clean, I think I'm going to have to get hooked into some really powerful meetings and stay in therapy. And I need to pay out-of-pocket for the things I get—and keep walking and exercising. I have to just really stay close to honesty and stay vigilant in some stuff that I still just struggle with. For example, I got caught doing something the other day, and my first reaction was that I wanted to make up this big story. It's just my first reaction, all the time. It's my learned reaction from when I was a little kid. My mom said I used to lie about things that didn't matter. She would say, "Did you take that orange?" And I would say, "No." She said, " I don't care if you took the orange, I just asked." Just as an example. I always thought I had to have a reason for everything I did.

I think it's an organic or genetic problem. I have a brother who's gay, and his is organic and genetic. When I've talked to him about it, he's told me that he's liked little boys from the time he was four or five. And I can remember my dad one time coming home, and my brother had a napkin on his head and was dancing, and my dad saying to my mom, "What's wrong with him?" He didn't play with trucks and he wasn't banging stuff. I had another brother who was banging holes in walls and just doing boy kind of stuff. My mom also said that she took a lot of diet pills while she was pregnant with me, because when she was pregnant back then they would prescribe diet pills because they didn't want women getting real heavy, so I don't know if that's a contributing factor or not.

Critical Thinking Questions

1. **What does the interviewee believe the reasons were behind her getting involved in delinquent behaviors? To what extent do you agree with her reasoning?**

2. **The title of this is "It Was the Rush!" What does that mean? Give examples out of the subject's life.**

3. **The interviewee had a number of "ups and downs" in her life. What were they, and how did she handle them?**

4. **In your opinion, is she now cured? What do you believe her chances are of staying out of further difficulties? What recommendations would you make to her if you were to meet her?**

5. **To what extent is she comfortable with her understanding of why she took the path she did?**

IT WAS THE FEAR!

When I was young, I was often plagued by distressing thoughts. Often, should I hear disturbing news or see a disturbing image on television, the images or sounds would linger long after the original were gone. The harder I tried to rid myself of them, the harder they clung to my mind and filled my waking moments. Though this is a rather normal phenomenon, my thoughts went further. I became, literally, obsessed with thoughts I thought were morally wrong. Forbidden blasphemous thoughts would fill my head as I tried, quite desperately, to force them out. I would worry about going to hell. I was terrified of my house catching on fire or my parents or sisters becoming hurt. My mind would involuntarily create hideous scenarios in which I had to choose between a family member or my favorite pet being thrown into a pit of fire simply because I did not want to think about these things. I would worry about small things, too. I would worry about say, my stomach growling in front of others.

To add to these thoughts, I would feel a vast and unappeasable compulsion to check the house irons, make sure light switches were off, check my shoes for trailing toilet paper, etc. Sometimes, lasting for months on end, certain compulsions would take me. I had to move my arm in a certain way, or raise my eyebrows, or move any number of muscles before I would feel better. And these had to be done almost every moment, whether or not I was absorbed in another task, only finding relief when I was sleeping or deeply involved in an activity. I went seventeen years, becoming a junior in high school, before I was finally diagnosed and given treatment for obsessive-compulsive disorder (OCD).

I didn't drink alcohol in high school. I was an oddball that way, but I managed to have fun without it. I still felt I was terribly inept in all social situations, but these were people I had known all my life and I could deal with them somewhat more easily. I had developed somewhat of a chip on my shoulder in my younger years and this kept me from making any real close friendships with all but a handful of people. I hoped college would be a great new start for me.

I began drinking in college. It was what everybody did, and to tell the truth, I had always been intimidated by those who drank and took drugs and wore dark, gothic clothing, and such. I believe that, in a way, my succumbing to alcohol and drug use was an attempt to rid myself of fear. There were fears I had no control over, such as those associated with my OCD, and those fears that I could confront. I was so sick of being afraid that I embraced everything I had the courage to. And alcohol and drugs and the lifestyle that accompanied them were easy to adopt.

I didn't start with drugs. Alcohol was my major downfall. I found that when I drank, my shyness went away and I could finally talk to people. I had no social phobias when I drank and I felt free and easy, so to speak. Of course, to get to this point, I had to drink past the tiredness stage, drink past the slightly tipsy but happy stage, and reach the inability to think and reason stage. And that was the best part. I didn't have to think. There were no worries, no obsessive thoughts, no inhibitions that I felt continuously over the years. I was free.

But that only lasted until the morning. Come morning, all the thoughts would come rushing back and I would be ashamed of everything I had done the night before. I wouldn't want to go to any of my classes and have to face those who I saw the night before. Many times I had to ask people what I had done the previous night. Or who I had done. And I could happily have stabbed myself from the shame.

I'm not sure if I ever had a real major depressive episode, for I cannot remember a lot of specifics, but I do know I lost all self-esteem and confidence in myself. Most days I didn't want to get out of bed—not until I could get another drink in me. If I could have slept through each day until it was "time" to drink again, I probably would have, and some days I even came close. I tried not to think during the day, or at least concentrate on non-personal issues such as television. I was ashamed to look most people in the eye and found myself at times spineless and at other times a "hardass." It all depended on who I was confronted with. But my world looked bleak most of the time. Being with my friends cheered me up, but it was dangerous for me to be by myself, without any distractions. So, again, I slept most of the day away, perhaps went to the gym, anything to get my mind off of life. I felt so hopeless I could physically feel my chest and my stomach hurt sometimes.

My obsessive religious thoughts literally plagued me the next day and I was sure I would be going to hell. One night, while drinking in a bar with a guy I was seeing, I sat alone in a corner with a lit cigarette while he played pool, and burned myself. Over and over I would hold the lit cigarette to my wrist until I could bear it no longer. I did this I told myself that this is what I deserved, I was a horrible person and I might as well get used to the fire now that I would live in for eternity.

I didn't really every care about school or anything else that was going on during college. Everything was about drinking and being with my friends. Though I didn't know it at the time, my friends were experiencing similar feelings of shame and worthlessness. One told me years later that, as well as sharing the feelings of shame and depression, she used to cut herself. I doubt we were the only ones.

One would imagine that after experiencing these feelings, the person in question would stop drinking. Only the opposite happened. I couldn't wait to get back those feelings of freedom and un-responsibility I felt. And so it would begin the next night. My friends and I drank, if not seven nights out of the week, at least five or six.

After a while I tried marijuana. Over all, I enjoyed pot the best because it made me laugh. I also did less crazy things than when I drank. But then I tried more serious drugs. It didn't happen immediately, but after a couple years of watching other sorority sisters being enraptured by ecstasy and coke, and extolling the "awesome" feelings they experienced, I tried them myself. For some reason, I never experienced the high everyone else did. I don't know whether it is some aspect of my brain chemistry that kept me from experiencing these, but I do know that it may have saved my life. I was so anxious to dissociate from my own reality that these powerful drugs, should they have worked, would have dragged me to depths of which I very probably would not have climbed out.

These "self-medicating" procedures went on after college. I had a full-time job and managed to keep it, but most days out of the week I was hung over until I left work. I would go to the bars myself if no one would come with me. One night I was drugged. I had taken a few drinks out of one beer and remembered nothing else. If it were not for some conscientious people present at the bar, a stranger would have succeeded in carrying me out of the bar. It is possible I would not have been seen again.

However, this *still* didn't stop me from drinking. Its pull was too powerful and it's usefulness for escape too seductive, as all drugs are. At this time, I started seeing another guy, but after a while my drinking began to create a rift in our relationship. I also began to realize that I didn't have anything to hope for; my job was so-so and my future in the business didn't seem alluring. I began to think about returning to school. I had sworn I would never do this, but suddenly I began to get a little flutter of excitement in my stomach. I decided I wanted to quit drinking, but for a couple years the most I could do was decrease the frequency with which I drank, but not the quantity. I also realized, fearfully and desperately, that I had forgotten how to have fun without alcohol. Any event I attended dimmed in its attractiveness compared to my thoughts of drinking afterward. I couldn't even throw a Frisbee without thinking of the beer that was available to be drunk. This aspect of forgetting how to have fun was probably the most intimidating and inhibiting factor to my quitting drinking for good.

Then one night, after drinking a rather large quantity at a local bar, I got in a fight with my boyfriend on our way home. I don't remember any of the events—it was another "blackout" night but I got angry and jumped from his moving vehicle. I dimly remember some aspects of the hospital, such as having a cat scan and my blood being taken, but for the most part I was still blacked out. That was the last night I ever took a drink.

The next few months, even the next two years, were not easy. I had to abandon some friends and find other interests to occupy my mind. Some nights the urge to drink made me cry. My parents and my boyfriend were the most important factors in my maintaining abstinence, but I also felt a tremendous, indescribable sense of relief the day I realized I would never again have another drink. I didn't every have to worry about not being in control of my actions again. I have to admit that it took almost a year and a half for me to re-learn. I'm still learning, too. When hard times hit, I get those old urges to drink. They're diminishing in intensity, though sometimes they flare up pretty fiercely. In those times I try not to think about the future. If I do that, the days of alcohol-freeness seem overwhelming and I find myself more easily succumbing to the idea of drinking. So I think about the moment and things I can do to occupy myself. I also focus on how I would feel if I woke up the next day and realized I had drunk the night before. I'm not ready for that guilt.

Critical Thinking Questions

1. **What role do you believe that having obsessive-compulsive disorder played in this young woman to fears.**

2. **What about OCD would lead a person to become depressed?**

3. **What was the attractiveness of drinking and drugs in this woman's early life?**

4. What were the downsides of drinking and rugs in her life?

5. How did this young woman mange to turn her life around? What appears to have happened?

PART II

PROFESSIONALS WHO WORK

WITH YOUTHFUL OFFENDERS

Ten statements from professionals are included in this section. Three police officers discuss police investigations and how they try to reduce the victimization of children through prosecution. A juvenile court judge communicates his concern for helping troubled children. A juvenile court officer defines the changing roles of probation officers. A staff member comments on working in a group home. A social worker shares her observations of working with female youthful offenders. A superintendent develops her philosophy of care and explains the program of a model county juvenile facility. A therapist who has worked with sex offenders describes a "worst case scenario," and how the case is approached. A founder of a rehabilitation center for women discusses some of the kinds of attitudes and behaviors of women who have passed through her facility. Finally, two highly placed professionals, one a former juvenile prosecutor and the other, the Deputy Commissioner of Probation in New York City, discuss their experience, the nature of their work, and how their respective departments cope with the problems of youths.

FORMER POLICE CHIEF ROGER CUCCARO, LT. KIRK HESSLER, AND SGT. RICHARD HORNER, POLICE INTERROGATION AND VICTIMIZATION

Police interrogation, as the following statement reflects, is an important aspect of police-juvenile relations.

On November 15, 1996, we traveled to a residence to investigate a theft case. The house was a known party house for juveniles and a hideout for juvenile runaways. Living in the house were four female children ages four, six, eight, and ten; two adult parents; and one male juvenile age seventeen, who was a ward of the young girls' parents.

After knocking on the rear door, the door was opened, and the smell of burning marijuana could be detected. Marijuana was in plain view on the kitchen table near the door. After getting consent to search the residence, more drug paraphernalia was discovered. Only the electric stove in the kitchen was heating the house. The house was in deplorable condition and unfit for adult habitation, let alone for children. The children's rooms contained four-inch-square unplugged holes in the walls where a porch roof used to be attached. The children's beds were next to these holes. The plumbing in the bathroom was inoperable. Garbage was piled up inside and outside the house. Children and Youth Services (CYS) was called to take custody of the four girls. The children were put into the care of their paternal grandparents by CYS.

Once in the custody of the grandparents, the children began talking to the grandmother about people at their home beating them, taping their mouths shut, and having sex with them.

The grandmother reported this to CYS. CYS notified the North Franklin Township Police Department, which set up interviews with the children. CYS also sent out notices to the suspects to tell them of the accusations.

The police and CYS jointly interviewed all four girls on several occasions. It was discovered that all of the girls had been victims of sexual assault on multiple occasions, sometimes by multiple assailants. The girls reported assaults by four individuals (an adult in his forties, an eighteen-year-old youth, a sixteen-year-old juvenile, and another seventeen-year-old juvenile who was the chief offender). Both agencies tape-recorded the interviews. (The DA's office later set up a protocol that forbids the tape-recording of child interviews.) Then the children were interviewed again. Some of the girls were again interviewed prior to each hearing. Additional information was developed during these interviews.

The assistance of CYS workers at the initial interviews was invaluable. They are excellent at creating rapport with small children and testing the truthfulness of a child in identifying body parts. Such interviews are especially difficult. Besides the need to create rapport so that children will speak to strangers about such incidents, the integrity of the child's memory must be maintained. The children were given counseling to lessen the impact of their experiences. Such counseling can dull the details of their memories, which would be counter to the objective of a criminal prosecution, in which accurate memories are needed.

Unfortunately, CYS also sent out notices to suspects. This works against police interviewers, who prefer to catch the suspects "cold," providing a different dynamic to the interview.

The investigators found that the home was a flophouse for drunks and drug abusers. The forty-year-old adult offender was a homeless person who came there to party; the eighteen-year-old stayed there off and on to get away from his own home; the sixteen-year-old came to party; the seventeen-year-old lived there as a ward of the victims' parents. Often the parents would throw parties attended mostly by juveniles who were given alcohol, marijuana, and cocaine. Sexual encounters between consenting juveniles were frequent. The young girls' parents would go out a few nights a week to drink and play dart ball, leaving the seventeen-year-old to baby-sit the children, and the pedophile orgies would begin. Quite often the participants would be drinking or smoking marijuana. The children would be called in the ward's bedroom, where they would be forced, at times with their mouths taped shut, to watch the babysitter having sex with one of the sisters. They would then get their turn in bed. Sometimes the other offenders would join in and have various types of sex with one of the girls. Some involved sexual touching or rubbing of genitals, and some involved penetration. The girls all reported nude pictures being taken of two of the sisters.

The sex ranged from penile penetration of the vagina and the anus to placing fingers in the vagina to masturbation of the victims. No oral intercourse was reported.

The suspects were questioned, and all denied the occurrences. The victims were medically examined. Some showed signs of penetration, and some did not. It is not uncommon for girls this age to heal physically after violation.

The parents denied any knowledge of the occurrences. The mother denied having knowledge of the photos, which the girls said they found and gave to the mother. The girls said that their mother beat the ward with a frying pan upon seeing the photos recovered from his room. She denied seeing the photos and said that she herself had been molested by her father and no one believed her.

A break came when the eighteen-year-old suspect confessed to having had sexual contact with one of the girls.

Four assailants were charged and the juveniles jailed or put into juvenile detention. The parents were charged with neglect and corruption-related charges. Charts were created for each offender to show who molested whom, and in what manner.

Two other juvenile boys were implicated when the girls recounted times when the ward would take them on walks in the woods with their male cousins and have them engage in mock sex acts. These boys were noted but not charged because investigators believed that their arrest would only serve to further complicate the case, and their charges would be relatively minor compared to those of the other suspects. Since each defendant was entitled to a hearing in which the victims would be required to testify, the four girls had to testify at least four times about their experiences.

The investigators took a statement from a juvenile in detention with the ward, who had been bragging to him about having sex with the little girls.

The two juvenile defendants were certified adult by the juvenile judge and were put into the county jail adult facility. After a year awaiting trial, the eighteen-year-old and the sixteen-year-old gave statements against the other assailants.

About one year after their removal from their parent's home, the young girls went to visit their maternal grandparents. While there, a neighbor of the grandparents molested two of the youngest. This fellow was arrested, and the girls testified at his trial. He was found guilty and jailed. This heightened our concern about facts from one case "bleeding into the other."

In summary, numerous problems were encountered in this case. First, the children had to be able to articulate what happened to them. Second, rapport had to be developed between them and the investigators. Third, CYS notified the suspects of the allegations prior to police contact; this destroyed the "surprise" effect used in typical investigations. Fourth, with so many actors and victims, "score" cards had to be created to keep track of who did what with whom and how it was done. Additionally, several other juveniles had to be located and questioned. These were youths who attended parties, or who the children saw having sex. Of course, most of these people did not remember anything about the alleged incidents. Even though some juvenile girls reported to their girlfriends that they were raped there while drunk or drugged, these victims would not confirm the reports.

Added to this mix was another molestation in a different jurisdiction. This led to the blending of stories, which made it even harder for the very young girls to distinguish the separate occurrences. Nevertheless, all offenders were found guilty.

Needless to say, everyone who came in contact with the case found it emotionally draining. The secretary typing the statements would become upset just listening to the statements while typing them. The investigators had to be more compassionate with these children, who quite often required hugs and reassurance. This was not typical cop behavior in dealing with victims.

The case took more than two years to complete. All four victims underwent counseling and appeared to be doing well seven years later. The officers in charge of the original case still occasionally ran into the two youngest children. These two appeared to be well-adjusted and happy children. One played softball in a summer league, and both were living with their parents and grandmother, who also appear to have pulled their lives together. The parents had undergone counseling at CYS and became involved closely with their children.

In April of 2005, however, the younger of the two girls, now sixteen, reported being raped again. One rape was by her ex-boyfriend, but she also was raped a number of times by an adult member of her family. Her parents had started camping with the girls and, one evening, as the younger sister walked from the campsite to the restroom, she was followed by this adult member of her family and raped. This family member then raped her a number of times during the summer and fall of 2005. The boyfriend's rape was not reported and was discovered as police officers interviewed her about the adult family member's rape.

This young girl apparently is unable to stay out of risky situations. She appears to have no physical characteristics or psychological demeanors that would identify her as a victim.

A Postnote: Rumors on the street indicate that one of the seventeen-year-olds found guilty was placed in a maximum-security adult prison where he was viciously gang-raped; he had to have a colostomy because of the rape. He now has served nine years of a twenty-two-year sentence.

Source: Information supplied by former Police Chief Roger Cuccaro, Lt. Kirk Hessler, and Sgt. Richard Horner of the North Franklin Police Department and unnamed sources. Updated May 2006.

Critical Thinking Questions

1. What are the characteristics of girls this young that would affect how they respond to interrogation?

2. What particular difficulties would you have if you were a police detective dealing with the molestations in this case?

3. To what extent should prosecutors and defense attorneys be permitted to question girls this age on the stand?

THE HONORABLE DANIEL BLOCK, JUVENILE COURT JUDGE

I grew up in a small town, and there wasn't a whole lot to do. In seventh grade we had to do a research paper in school on a career that interested us, and mine was on a lawyer. I knew by then that I wanted to go to law school. Believe it or not, I still got into a little bit of trouble here and there along the way, which piqued my interest in the legal system. The local police officer handled all of the juvenile court cases. It made me interested in the process when I realized how much discretion the police officer has. The most critical decisions in the whole legal process is that initial charging decision. As I look back on it, I wouldn't be sitting here right now if that police officer had treated me differently on many separate occasions. But he chose not too.

As a juvenile court judge, the best part of my job is to see change in children. They tease me at times about whether I am giving lecture one, two, or three, but the kids do listen. On a weekly basis, I see someone who will say, "Do you remember me? You had me in court." They go on to tell me what is going on in their lives. I run into a lot of parents in the community. I ran into a grandmother at the grocery store the other day who asked me whether I remembered that I took away her grandchild. The child is back home now, is doing well, and it was the best thing that ever happened to him. I live for those moments.

The hardest part of my job is sending children back home after you release them or more frequently taking them out of a foster home where they have done well, back to a home in which they had problems before. The parents have done everything you have asked them to do to get their kids back, but thirty days, forty days, six months later the kids are using drugs again. All the old problems have resurfaced.

Some come into court and tell me that relapse is a step toward recovery. When I started prosecuting in the county attorney's office in 1990, crack cocaine was just plaguing this community. I was removing almost a baby a week born to a mother on crack cocaine. I was prosecuting fifteen- and sixteen-year-olds for selling crack cocaine on the streets. Possession to deliver is a Class D Felony. A lot of those kids were being waved into the district court.

However, the law has now changed. If you are sixteen years old and get caught with crack cocaine, you begin in the district court. I used to think that crack cocaine was going to be the end of our civilization or the end of our society as we know it. I probably see one crack cocaine case a month these days. It is now methamphetamine. I am removing one meth baby every week or maybe one every two weeks. To me, methamphetamine is much more serious than cocaine because I believe it causes life-long neurological damage to both those who use it and the children exposed to it. Another problem, as far as drugs go, is it is relatively cheap on the streets. It is so readily accessible because you have all those people out there that can make it.

In my courtroom, I have had meth labs in basements, meth labs in garages, meth labs in trunks of cars, and meth labs in boats on the river. I do have to say that law enforcement is getting a little grasp on controlling it. Law enforcement is making it more difficult to buy a lot of the ingredients in large quantities, especially over-the-counter drugs.

Another of the attorneys here and I recently had a discussion about this. We questioned what will be the drug of choice for the next decade. We have had crack cocaine and gotten control of that. It is meth now. Perhaps, it will be Ice tomorrow. Ice has not been a big thing for me in the juvenile court, but I know that there will be something else coming.

Another change is I think we are definitely getting different kids now than we got ten years ago. They are more violent and more damaged for a lot of reasons. Methamphetamine is one. Two, we have fewer resources for kids now than we did ten years ago. What it all comes down to is money. When I first came to Black Hawk County, I was amazed at the resources we had for kids. Now, there aren't many of these resources left for delinquent children.

I feel that we have become much more reactive than proactive. I am forced to respond to what the kids are doing rather than choosing from the diversion services in our community. I'm seeing kids who are third generation in my courtroom. I see the thirty-four-year-old grandmother in court, who came before me as a child. Her children and now her grandchildren are in my courtroom. A lot of these families have long histories of substance abuse. They have not realized the value of education.

I try to hold myself apart as the educational judge. When I walk into the courtroom, the least expectation that I have of that kid is that he or she will get at least a GED. I'm told that when you are eighteen years old, even McDonald's won't hire you anymore without a high school diploma.

When I have parents in court, I always say, "Mr. and Mrs. Jones, is there anything the juvenile court can offer to assist your son or daughter?" And they will say, "We don't want him hanging around with so and so." To me, when my parents told me that I couldn't hang around with some kid, who was the first kid I ran to when my parents weren't looking?

In response, you say, "Jimmy, the first term on the probation contract is—always obey the rules of the parents." I don't want to be the parent. A lot of the parents who come in want me to be the heavy and the disciplinarian. They want me to be the person who says, "No." I don't want to absolve the parent of that duty.

There is another difference I have witnessed since I first started doing the job of an assistant county attorney. I would probably see one girl to every ten male delinquents. If it isn't 50-50 now, it is at least 40-60. Why? I call it the Cinderella syndrome. None of these girls have ever been told, "No." All of a sudden, they get to be fourteen or fifteen, and the teacher in high school or the parents start to say, "No." The girls refuse to go to school. They are having sexual relations when eighteen and nineteen years old. They are smoking. Their parents now realize that they have to say, "No." But it can't be done.

I would take ten of the hardest delinquent boys to one of these delinquent girls. I can't tell you how many times they tell me, "Send me away until I am eighteen, and then when I am eighteen, I can do whatever I want."

I do have some options. We have some excellent foster and community-based programs for girls. The problem is that you take the kid out of the environment, give the kid all the skills to be successful, and you put them back into the same environment.

So, you get the kid all shiny, like a brand new penny, and it is just a matter of time before they are back to where they were before. Within sixty days, boom, the kid has the same old problems. There are a few exceptional cases in which the kids can open up their eyes and see what is good for them. They can see where they have been, can see where they are going, and can see the benefits of the treatment they have received. They can put all their skills to work, but the majority falls back into the old patterns of behavior.

I get so frustrated because funding sources won't pay for therapy for the family. For example, the federal government won't pay for therapy for the family because they say that we are paying for therapy for the kid. How does a kid get the way he got?

When I started, we did about one parental termination case per year; we now do one or two a month. I think that this is better for kids. We used to have kids in foster care for three or four years. The thinking was to give parents more and more time to get themselves together. Now, we are looking at kids' needs as well as parents'.

I personally believe that lawyers for children are more important than even lawyers for adults. Kids don't know the process. Kids don't understand the consequences. I think kids are better off to have someone who does all juvenile work. The juvenile court is such a specialized area. It is hard to step into juvenile court and meet all the needs of the child, the court, and the process. The typical child assistance case has the county attorney, DHS social workers, providers who work with DHS, mom, mom's attorney, dad, dad's attorney, the guardian *ad litem*, and maybe even grandma or grandpa, aunt or uncle. You have all those players. There is a need for a specialized court, a need for a specialized law practice.

I am concerned about the future of the juvenile court for a lot of reasons. Money is the root of it. I operate on a couple different money streams. One funds the residential treatment program; another funding stream authorizes me to pay for community-based treatment. Right now, in Black Hawk County, we have about a twenty-one-child waiting list for a child to go to residential treatment. If your child came into the courtroom today, was smoking crack cocaine, and was running away from home, and you said that you couldn't do anything with him, I would have to tell the parent, "By the way, he will be number twenty-two on the list, and my best guess is it will be six or seven months before Jimmy can go to treatment."

However, immediate consequences are necessary when you are dealing with kids. What I do is try to band-aid the situation. I send the kid to youth shelter until he gets fed up and runs away from there and is out using again. Then, he commits a law violation, and I can lock him up in detention until we have space for him in residential treatment. Now, how is that in the community's best interest? I have spent a hundred and some dollars for the youth shelter and a hundred and fifty dollars a day on detention. I have completely drained my community-based funds. I can't even pay for UA's [urine analysis] right now. We have no money, because I've been trying to maintain the kids until I can get a residential placement.

I like kids and enjoy working with them. Even with the limitations of resources, I am able to do what I think is in the best interest of the child. I want kids to feel safe in my courtroom. I enjoy having the interaction with the kids and their parents. I've been accused of doing family therapy in court, but a lot of times I try to get the issues on the table, so we can talk about them. It is a very rewarding career.

Critical Thinking Questions

1. **Has this juvenile court judge said anything that surprised you?**

2. **What does he say are the most rewarding aspects of his job?**

3. **What are the most frustrating aspects of his role as a juvenile court judge?**

4. **Would you like to be a juvenile court judge?**

5. **What would you tell adolescent girls who argue they should be able to do anything they want?**

RUTH FRUSH, CHIEF JUVENILE COURT OFFICER

I started at Juvenile Court Services right out of college and was a secretary for a year. Then I became a probation officer, and I did that for twenty-five years. In the last eight months, I became chief probation officer of this judicial district.

In the twenty-five years I was a probation officer, probation changed a lot. For one thing, the philosophy has changed. Initially, I worked with diversion cases, and my case load was thirty. When I became chief this past July, my case load had increased to three hundred. It used to be that if a child was not conforming to probation expectations, the best thing was to place him or her out of the home, either in short-term shelter care or in long-term group care. Now, the philosophy is that these types of out-of-the-home placements are not necessarily getting us the growth we want, and so we are working more to keep kids in their homes.

When I first started, I was a caseworker, and, more or less, I did it all. I got the kid up and took him to school if that was what was needed. By the time I had become chief, we had nearly become case managers. We now hire people to do a lot of our tracking, to get kids where they need to be. We do a lot more paperwork and case-management types of things, and most of that has to do with the increased number of cases we have.

One of the best things that has happened in this time frame is restorative justice. I am a firm believer in restorative justice. Victims do need to be acknowledged and have some say in what happens with the system. Restitution has been very beneficial for the victims but also for the kids, with the accountability aspect. We say, "This is the damage you have done." What better way than to have a person pay for damage and expense and to take ownership for their behavior?

Communities have stepped up and said, "We want some accountability from the youth." I think victims have stepped up and asked for more input in the system, in terms of how things should look and what should happen to kids. The community service part where kids work in the community has been very beneficial, both for the kids and for the community.

One of my jobs used to be to take groups of kids out where we would paint fire hydrants. We worked on picnic tables and cleaned all the city parks' bathrooms for years. You can bet that when you are taking a group of kids around and they would see a fire hydrant, some one would say, "You see that hydrant? We painted that last summer."

They would take more pride in their community and things they have done. I have heard them say to other kids, "Don't be painting on that floodwall any more. I just painted that, and I don't want to have to go and paint it again." The work program has had quite an impact on them.

The way we handle things has also affected probation. Now, when they are sixteen and commit a forcible felony, they actually go to jail. They don't go to the detention center They start out in the adult system. Personally, I would like to see a Youthful Offender Law, where we could work with them in our system and, if they don't quite get it, we could move them up to the adult system. Or if they were obstinate and refused to cooperate with the juvenile system, we could bump them up to the adult system.

I am a firm believer that kids can change. They can learn from their mistakes. It takes some a little longer than it does others. Sometimes, you are called to make some hard judgments. You know that you may work with them in juvenile court, but when they turn eighteen, they go into the adult system. Or they may be better off to be in the adult system, with a longer time frame, and you may have better results. It is a hard judgment call! It has definitely changed the look of some of the kids we have been working with.

Overall, kids are kids. We do have some difficult cases now, a lot of mental health issues. In the past, we didn't acknowledge them as much or perhaps they weren't there in the numbers they are now.

Family dynamics and community support has also changed through the years. When I first started, the family had a kind of respect for law enforcement and probation, and you don't necessarily see that now.

Kids today have access to a variety of drugs. We had our concern with drugs back then, but it has changed a lot. Meth and some of the new stuff result in such bizarre behavior. We don't see a high percentage of cases on meth, but the cases we do see are very difficult cases. One part of it is that the kids exhibit rather bizarre behavior; the other part is the high rates of failure. Most of the cases we work with have gone through treatment at least twice. It is so hard for the family, as well as the kid, to come to grips with their addictive behaviors.

The best part of being a probation officer is working with kids. Periodically, you have kids come back and say, "I got my GED. I'm the only one out of the six kids in my family to get my GED." It is really rewarding. I still have some young ladies who come back here and bring their last child in to show me and things like that. You have to learn to adjust your standards and be able to celebrate the little things with people.

We do hold some high expectations of kids, perhaps a lot higher than their parents. We do expect that they comply with curfew, that they will be in school, and that they meet the expectations they have agreed in their contract to do.

We do give kids a lot of resources to help them fulfill their obligations. We do a lot of work with the schools to keep them in school. I feel that we give them a lot of assistance along the way, but no doubt we do hold them to a higher expectation than the average child on the street.

We are working on a risk assessment now, which should be up and going this summer. It should be helpful in terms of rating kids as low, medium, and high risk—risk to the community and risk of reoffending. I am hoping that this risk assessment will help us match kids with programs better, community programs, residential treatment programs, or the training school. We want to be able to better match resources with our kids and to do the best job we can.

The training school is sometimes the best resource for those kids who have reached the end of our resources. Most of these kids have been through at least one group home and day treatment. If you can get the kid matched up to the right resource, then good things can happen. A lot of it depends on what the family will buy into. I have kids who say, "My older brother and my dad are in prison, and I am going in there anyway, so who cares."

We are not sending kids out of state, because it is very costly. In our service area, we only have one kid we have sent out of state. He is in Texas. We sent him because nobody in the state of Iowa would take him, and he was too young for the training school.

We get a lot of grief, in a lot of different ways. And there is some danger. Early on, I had a young man in my office, and we were battling verbally over his going to work crew. He wouldn't leave my office. He was between the door and me, and I couldn't leave the office. I picked up the phone to call the sheriff's office, and he left. On another occasion, following a court hearing, we took a young man to his home. We read in the paper the next day that the police investigated the apartment where we had dropped the young man and confiscated a number of guns. We had gone into the apartment, and it gave us a funny feeling because it had fifteen or twenty people in it, and it was a small apartment. They were decent to us, but to read that in the paper was a little intimidating.

We have also had staff members who had their hair pulled. We almost had a car accident; a girl in handcuffs grabbed the driver and pulled her head down so she couldn't see. The driver was able to stop the car, but the girl got out and jumped over a fence. We have had a couple incidents in which staff and kids had altercations in the parking lot.

Many of our cases are not easy. Back in the mid-1980s, we had a young man who got into a fight with another young man over a girl. He hit the guy once, broke his nose, and killed him. We opted not to send this young man to the training school. As part of probation, he paid for the funeral, which cost $4,666. He worked every minute he could and paid that off, because his family had no money. He just could never forgive himself. Alcohol eventually took over his life, and he died at a young age.

A couple years ago I had a vehicular homicide case in which a youth was charged in juvenile court. The accident actually happened in August, and he was sixteen at the time. He and I worked through a lot of things. He did everything we asked of him. On the other side of that, I worked with the victim of the accident, who would have graduated from college that spring. He had not been drinking that night, and he was going to take over the family business. His parents were going away to be missionaries, which had been the plan for years. He had a long-time girlfriend. The family's whole life was just turned about.

So, we did the waiver of jurisdiction hearing, since the kid was just sixteen. The court let him finish off the school year in the community, and then they sent him off to adult prison. That was by far the hardest case I ever worked. We couldn't discuss it much because it wouldn't have been appropriate, because of the legal stuff. But you could see it all over him. In adult court, after the family had the opportunity to speak up to this young man, he actually apologized to them. He said, "If I could, I would switch places with your son." I believed him. My hope is that his going into prison will give him a little time to forgive himself. The last I heard he is doing well and taking some college courses. He should be out in another six years.

Let me conclude by saying that probation has been a very good career for me. There are a lot of good aspects to probation. You work with a variety of people. It also gives you a good perspective on your own life and your own children. It is very interesting. No two days are ever the same. Some days you hit the door, and you think you know what you are going to do, and it just doesn't go that way. You build a lot of relationships, and you figure out how to work with people. You are constantly using your mind to sort things out and to figure out if there is a better way. It is a very challenging and taxing job. You have to be confident in your values and what you believe. You have to have thick skin. It does take a lot of your heart and soul. You need to be comfortable with who you are.

If you are interested in working in this field, I would suggest that you volunteer in juvenile justice areas. Work with some of those kids, their parents, and people in the field. Get as much experience as you can. Some of that might involve working at a Youth Shelter or detection center. Get as much experience as you can.

Critical Thinking Questions

1. **How, according to this statement, has probation changed in the last couple of decades?**

2. **Would you like to work as a juvenile probation officer? Do you see yourself as a person with the personal characteristics to be an effective juvenile probation officer?**

3. **What aspects of the job would you find challenging and fulfilling?**

4. **What aspects of the job would you find difficult and frustrating?**

ROBERT QUIRK, A STAFF MEMBER'S PERSPECTIVE ON A GROUP HOME

It seems to me that the two most important considerations of the child care worker's job are to work effectively with residents and to develop a good relationship with staff. Firstly, there are a number of characteristics that we must possess as effective child care workers. We must have the respect of residents. We earn residents' respect by demonstrating confidence in our ability to handle the situations we face every day. We earn residents' respect by refusing to be intimidated and by not allowing them to give us verbal abuse. We earn their respect by being wise to the games they play and not permitting them to manipulate us. We earn their respect when we are fair and consistent in dealing with them. Finally, we earn their respect when holding them accountable for their behavior.

Secondly, in order to be an effective child care worker, you must have your own "stuff" together. What this means is that we cannot be on the job to fulfil our own needs; we must be there to help residents fulfil their needs and become responsible in their behaviors. Workers who are insecure, who have too great a need to be liked, or who have to rescue residents will not last.

Third, the best child care workers are perceptive, sensitive, patient, and compassionate. They have the ability to read the residents and to see through the "fronting" or putting on an act. They seem to operate on a gut feeling level and are continually able to sense what is really going on with residents. They are patient with the struggles of residents. They know that it has taken sixteen years or so for residents to develop their problems, and they are not likely to change overnight. They are caring individuals and are able to communicate this caring to their charges.

Another part of being an effective child care worker is developing a good relationship with other staff. A good relationship is based on respect. You earn the respect of other staff members the same way that you earn the respect of residents. Workers despise weak co-workers as much as, if not more than, residents despise weak staff. It is necessary to pick up the "slack" caused by weak co-workers as well as to deal with the frequent problems they create.

A good relationship with other staff is harmed when a staff member does not follow through with enforcing the rules or confronting residents' behaviors. This is particularly seen with those who have the need to be rescuers. Rescuers typically minimize behaviors and allow excuses for behaviors. They turn their backs on rule violations and don't follow through on consequences given by others. If there is a rescuer in the chain of workers, the residents will use this weak link to their advantage.

It is also hard to work with those who are inconsistent, especially when it is intentional. Staff members sometimes have a secret agenda, which refers to a co-worker attempting to obtain goals other than those developed by the team or agency. This can also occur when a co-worker attempts to reach established goals in a different manner than what was developed by the team.

Another problem with co-workers results from a staff member who is able to function only when things are black and white and is unable to deal with grey areas. If these co-workers are confronted with a problem for which there is no specific rule, they are lost and do not know what to do. When you remember that a great deal of the problems we face lie in the grey areas where there are no specific rules, it becomes clear why such staff members create the problems they do.

A final co-worker problem is caused by supervisors who either are out of touch with the residents or do not accept the input of child care workers who are in direct contact with residents and know them the best. These supervisors then make poor policy and treatment decisions. This creates alienation, lowers morale, and simply makes the job so much harder.

Critical Thinking Questions

1. **Based on Robert Quirk's statements, what do you think he likes about his job?**

2. **What do you think is most frustrating for him?**

3. **Does a job in a juvenile residential program sound attractive to you as a career option?**

RITA FERNAU, SOCIAL WORKER AT QUAKERDALE

I went to work in a private agency in Des Moines called "Children and Families of Iowa." I started to work with girls at the Iowa Juvenile Home and was then hired by a non-profit to develop community-based programs. I developed two female community-based programs in Newton, Iowa. That was at the time that they were taking the Mitchellville Girls Reformatory and moving the girls to Toledo, so that they could become the Women's Reformatory, in the early 1980s. As time went on, we opened up another female program in Newton, which was the first female sex program for adolescence.

I worked for Children and Families of Iowa for eighteen or twenty years and then was approached by Quakerdale to take over the Waterloo campus. The Waterloo campus was co-ed, and I accepted the position with the stipulation that we would have an all-female campus. This has always been a dream of mine to have three levels of care in one place, in order to work with young women. They agreed with that, and the rest is history.

We have three levels of care—we have day treatment consisting of an after school program for teenage adolescents, two comprehensive programs with ten girls in each unit, and a transitional living program for older girls who are working for independence. There are six girls in that cottage, and it is kind of like a college dorm setting. There are expectations, but they have their own food, TVs in their room, and they have to work part time and complete their education. They do a lot of skill building about being independent, budgeting, job search and interviews, and things like that.

We take young women here from twelve to eighteen. There are twenty-six girls who are here, twenty-four seven. We also take pregnant girls. We bring them in, and one of the staff will become their Lamaze partner. We have two options: specialized foster homes that have agreed to work with us and who will take the babies when they are born, with the stipulation they have to work with the mother. So the adolescent girl may end up spending weekends and evenings there. The stipulation is that, unless it is a safety issue, the foster parents do not touch the baby. The young woman starts dealing early with the reality of being a mother.

We have had a couple of young women give the children up and a couple have kept them, sending them home with grandma or mom. We have had five or six go through the pregnancy program. We have one now, with the possibility of another coming in.

The differences in working with boys and girls center around relationships. The girls' whole world revolves around relationships. Our task or job is to keep these boundaries healthy. It takes a long time for girls to trust. You have to understand that the girls we deal with are court ordered. They are not here because they like us or want to be here, but sometimes they end up staying here because they like us. That is part of the reason why I wanted three or four levels of care. So many times we get these young women to the point of being successful, and they bottom out because they don't want to leave.

People sometimes ask me, "This girl has had five out-of-home placements. Why are you being successful with her? She has run from other placements, and she has done this and she has done that." The only thing I can say is that we make them feel safe. Part of this is that this is a female environment. We put young women in co-ed facilities, and if they have been raped or abused, and 99 percent of the time it has been with a male, they do not feel as safe. With young women, the sensitivity thing needs to be nurtured and not shut down.

I am not saying that my staff is running around and hugging the girls twenty-four hours a day. You have to be open enough to show some warmth to develop a relationship. With all the expectations we have put on youth care workers and the fear they have about touching a kid and hugging them, there is a knee-jerk reaction they have to approaching kids.

I have not taken a hard-core sex offender in the programs here, because you have to be highly skilled to work with hard-core sex offenders. We cannot be all things to all people. I believe that a lot of agencies and programs thought that they were, and they take a lot of risk in taking sex offenders when they don't know how to deal with them.

We have had young women who were forced to prostitute themselves to survive, and I am not white washing anything they do. But I really believe that terminology is very important.

A lot of the girls we have worked with have had substance abuse problems. I have a lot of trouble calling them addicts because a lot of the young women get into situational drug usage, if for no other reason than to self-medicate. Once we get rid of the issues they are trying to medicate, they usually don't have a lot of drug usage any more.

When a young lady comes into our program for the first time, normally from a juvenile court officer/DHS worker, we ask for a packet on the girl's background. I will say that there are very, very few women that we have ever turned down. We deal with a lot of cutters. We deal with a lot of mental health issues. We have to look at the risk factors. Even with the cutters, we look for the issue. What is the cutting covering up? What is the cutting substituting for?

We review the paper material. We may review again with the worker, and we meet as a clinical team. I have two licensed mental health therapists on staff. I have a couple of MA level who are working on their license, and all our RCs or line workers must have at least a BA in the social work field.

The staff and I look real close at the makeup of what we have. If we have an opening in one of the cottages, we have to look not only at the kid coming in but also at the kids who are already in the cottage. If we have five cutters in that cottage, I don't think it would be too smart to take another one. You also have to take into consideration maintaining staff's sanity. If there is any family at all, we try to engage the family.

The girls come in so angry and so defensive, and my staff are well-trained in not buying into those power struggles that the girls are so good at setting up, that I don't need to talk with the girls right away. If the girls continue to push wrong buttons, then I have a talk with them.

We had a runaway the other day. They brought her back, and she came up to me and said, "Miss Rita, are you mad at me?" I said, "Why should I be mad at you?" "I ran," she said. And I responded, "Why should I be mad at you? It is your life you're screwing up, not mine. If you start messing with my life, then I might get angry." She just looked at me and didn't know what to say. This was not the response she expected.

Kids try to force us into a box, and they try to force us to give them answers now. Kids come up to me and say, "Miss Rita, am I going to pass my week this week? Am I going to get my visit?" I just turn around and look at them and say, "I don't know. Are you? You know what your behavior has been all week better than I do."

The average length of stay here is ten to twelve months. A lot of that depends on where they are going when they leave and if they have any place to go.

We don't fight the family situation. I feel that bad breath is better than no breath at all. So, no matter what I think of their family, it is still their family. And these kids care about their families. We do a lot of family therapy; we do a lot of interaction and engagement with families. We may never be able to change mom, but we can instil in her daughters the skills to survive in that environment. There are a lot of very responsible people in this world who were raised by very crappy parents.

I think the really unique thing about what we do is that we have a great program that focuses on young women and empowers young women. Most programs take a girl in and try to fit her in the program. They have a little square box, and they try to put the kid in that box. I would like to think we take the girl and wrap the program around the girl and the program she needs.

Let me tell you how I interview people for a job here. When I interview people, the first thing I say to them is, "You're going to be working with some of the toughest young women in the state of Iowa for the least amount of pay and crappy hours. Do you want to go on with this interview?" I then say to them, "If you want a job, go to John Deere. You'll have better hours and more money. What I have here and what I need is a commitment to young women that are here." I don't say to them, but sometimes I think I should say, "And please have your own crap taken care of before you come to work here." I want somebody with common sense, some good life experience, and some commitment.

Critical Thinking Questions

1. **What did you learn about young women who are offenders or have mental health issues from this statement?**

2. **Why do you think that this program has been so effective with working with young women?**

3. **What type of staff members work well in this program? How do you think you would do?**

TERESA WISE, SUPERINTENDENT OF THE COUNTY HOME SCHOOL

I came to the County Home School in 1979 because I always had an interest in working with teens and there was an opening in the Business Office. I came without youth work experience beyond a little coaching and with an incomplete undergraduate degree. While working in the facility's business office, I had many opportunities to interact with the kids. I could talk with them as I handled their bank deposits from the work program and restitution activities. I also had some problem-solving responsibilities with the parents of the residents around clothing and money. I really enjoyed those interactions and saw first-hand how rejected these youth felt by society.

This motivated me to make a major career lane-change in my thirties and go back to college to get the credentials for future direct youth service job promotions. I completed my undergraduate degree in Youth Studies, Sociology/Corrections and later a Master's of Education.

I'm currently the superintendent of the County Home facility. We are a local county-run facility about ten miles from a major metropolitan city in the upper Midwest. The facility has a secure residential license for detention and internal support, a residential treatment license with staff secure components, and a certification from the State to treat juvenile sex offenders. It is licensed to serve 172 boys and girls between the ages of twelve and twenty with the average age being sixteen. This age range in itself is a challenge, but the physical plant layout helps. This facility has seven twenty-four bed cottages and a Transitional Living Center that are spread out over 170 acres. This allows for program separation based on age, risk, and specialized populations. The programs all share central space and some services like school, recreational fields, family therapy rooms, medical services, chaplaincy services, a horse barn, and a lake.

There's no fence around this facility, yet we had no escapes last year from the grounds of the facility. I attribute this accomplishment to the high quality of staff/resident relationships and respect for each other, good boundaries with residents, appropriate role modeling, and an overall understanding by staff that security and treatment are equally important.

Commitment decisions in the past were based mainly upon the seriousness of the youngster's instant offense, which often consisted of felony property and person offenses along with multiple gross misdemeanors. Thus, the focus of treatment was on commitment offenses. Today, most of the residents are committed to the facility because they are at high risk to reoffend based on a Youthful Level of Service Inventory (YLSI).

We believe that it's important that youngsters take responsibility for the behavior that led them here, but we do not end there, we begin there. Not only is the youth involved but, also the parent/guardian, probation officer, and community. Members of the community and parents are at the facility daily, and we receive 96 percent participation in developing treatment plans. We have geography on our side, but that alone does not account for this successful involvement. It is a core value of course to do anything necessary to make it happen, including using cabs for transportation.

It is not easy to work with parents and guardians. It is not easy to partner with multiple agencies. It's not easy when other agencies come in and look at what you're doing and then question why you are doing what you are doing. It is not easy to know that there are people who can say anything they want, and we may not be able to respond. This is both scary and healthy. I now know that this level of community involvement may be the most important change we made because now we have community ownership of the issues and community support. This year alone there will be ten scholarships from the community awarded at graduation.

One of the most significant changes over the years is that most of the residents have a mental health diagnosis in addition to Chemical Dependency and Conduct Disorder. Staff understands that the residents are both dangerous and vulnerable and are trained to work with youth who need protection and who, at the same time, are assaultive. So even though some of the language, the tools, and many of the ways we work with kids has changed, some of the core principles remain the same.

We are working with youngsters who have problems with their families, yet sometimes the kids are the healthiest person in the family. We have youth who cannot remember one good experience with school, and others have not attended school at all. They are not the joiners, the cheerleaders, the gymnast, football or basketball players, or on the track team. They have had no positive recreational experiences.

I don't think I am painting a picture of some unusual youth who is sent out of home today as every facility is coping or working with youth with multiple problems. So what do you do? Well, first staff must believe in change themselves. Sounds simple, but it's the important first ingredient.

I have seen staff who believe the opposite and think their duty is to contain youths for public safety. This belief and approach not only fails to work, but it also does not protect the public. Our programs are only as good as the staff, and I know we have a head up on other placements because the centerpiece of treatment—social learning—has never changed over the past twenty-five years. Other interventions, of course, have been added.

We do not believe that youngsters are born to commit crimes. Rather, they learned to make poor, harmful, and dangerous decisions through their life experiences. The role models they had or did not have and the life experiences they had or did not have were significant in who they became. And if they became this person through life events and adult modeling, then their lives can change.

I sometimes tell our new staff in orientation that if we were to make a movie of the lives of some of the youth who are committed here, no one would be able to watch the movie. Their lives have been that difficult. The attitudes our staff bring to work, how they engage with the kids, and whether or not they build relationships with the youngsters have a lot to do with whether or not the kids will change and whether that treatment will be effective.

The relationship-building is even more important in work with our young women. It is extremely important for men assigned to the girls program to have clear boundaries with the girls

88

and be up front by talking about professional relationships and not sexual relationships. This is important because we have examined the profiles of the girls who are committed to our program, and 86 percent have been sexually abused, and often by older men.

Every aspect of treatment with girls as well as boys must be tied to change and building community supports so the juveniles can be successful. Research identifies the parent as the most important figure in youth development. Relapse prevention is critical, and a plan should include recreation, school attendance, spirituality, and application of the skills built while in the facility to an on-the-job experience.

You cannot ignore chemical dependency. A lot of our youngsters are chemically dependent, so we have an on-grounds chemical dependency program. You cannot ignore mental health so, each program has two therapists, the facility has a consulting child and adolescent psychiatrist, and we don't just give the teens meds. We address the underlying issues. Addressing youngsters' mental health helps stabilize them so they are available for cognitive behavioral interventions.

We target interventions with the youngsters based on YLSI results giving all youth core programming. All the residents complete the cognitive "Thinking for a Change" program and experience quality education a full six hours a day. We support the academic school, so that if a resident's behavior regresses, he is taken out of school but is returned quickly. I have had special education teachers tell stories of teaching in public school settings, where the teacher can only teach for five minutes in a forty-five-minute class. Here at County Home School, where the kids feel safe and staff and teachers believe the residents can succeed, they can teach forty minutes in a forty-five-minute period.

The biggest satisfaction in this line of work is when you get an opportunity to see a former resident succeed. Last month I went to Saint Thomas University in St. Paul Minnesota to see their Humanitarian Award bestowed on one of our community partners. The award itself was great, but I also saw two former residents. There they were, dressed up in suits, in attendance just like me to see the presentation of an award to someone who obviously was their role model. They had been out for five years, were working, and doing quite well. I mean there's nothing better that this to give staff energy!

It's important to remember to celebrate. Celebrations are a big source of satisfaction for everyone. Celebrate even the small success! Remember to reward the big successes. We make certain that we celebrate our youngsters' graduation from high school upon receiving their GED. We have been doing this year after year. We graduate not only the residents who are still at the facility, but also any youth who was released any time that previous year.

Why do we ask them to come back? Because many of the kids and their parents do not have a place outside of here where they can celebrate this great achievement. They can be proud here. We also do this because it energizes the rest of the kids. It makes the current population believe they can do it too.

We also bring the alumni back. This kind of motivation cannot be matched with our words along. It gives the staff and kids a positive boost for days and weeks after the event. It is the kind of excitement that staff needs to continue with the energy it takes to work in this field.

I love it when something accidentally takes place that confirms the value of what we are doing. This can happen many ways, but it might be during a judicial tour of the facility. We randomly have sat down in the dining room across from a youth over lunch. The judge asks the youth a question about what happens in here and what has the child gained from his or her experience. Then youngster goes on to talk about his/her feeling of being safe, his/her relationship with the staff, telling about the humane environment, and people who care for him and want him to grow, change, and succeed. You can't beat this!

There are a lot of things here that make a difference. The children get breakfast in the morning. They're not worried that they're going to be harmed on the way to school. We are able to provide their basic needs that society should be able to provide every youngster in the community. Our youngsters are often experiencing their basic needs being met for the very first time in their lives. What further excites me is that we do not dehumanize our kids by looking at them as delinquents, criminals, or inmates. They're kids, and when you can see them as kids, you get excited and believe in change.

There are some similarities and differences between working with boys and working with girls. I talk a lot about relationship-building with the girls. The most important thing is that you don't go in acting like an expert. You learn to listen, and by dong so you are engaging them in their own treatment. Many of the girls ran away from home when they were very young; they have been on the street, used and dominated by men and gangs.

The girls will not act out as the boys do. Girls are more prone to self-mutilation and self-harmful behavior. The girls make up 14 percent of the admissions but 50 percent of all suicide evaluations. Take Monday, for example, when I had a girl who wouldn't eat breakfast or lunch and kept saying that everything was fine, but you knew it wasn't.

I do not want to say that relationships are unimportant to the boys. The boys' response is just much different. They want to be tough. One of my favorite young men when he first came to the institution took his shirt off all the way down to bare his chest. He was acting like this was an adult prison, to show the rest of the boys that he is tough. This behavior is learned and has to be unlearned. So many times we have handled these aggressive boys by putting more punishments on them. The reason why punishment doesn't work is because these kids are used to punishment and are not used to rewards. The biggest reason why punishment doesn't work is that they are immune to it.

I think that in this facility damage to kids can happen, and we always have to be vigilant. You know that even in the best hospitals adverse things can take place. I think that I would be naïve to believe no damage occurs. Having said this, let me say that we are committed to having a positive effect on kids. We believe and know that we do a lot of good for youngsters, and we monitor our work.

Critical Thinking Questions

1. Why do you think this facility is so well regarded in Minnesota and in other states?

2. How is this institution different from most juvenile institutions for youthful offenders?

3. How would it feel to work in a facility in which the superintendent is so passionate and excited about what she does and what the institution is accomplishing?

DOMENICK A. LOMBARDO, FORMER SUPERVISOR OF PSYCHOLOGICAL SERVICES, YOUTH DEVELOPMENT CENTER AT NEW CASTLE, PENNSYLVANIA

Let us consider a seventeen-year-old Caucasian, male, with an extensive history of psychiatric hospitalization. Although his criminal history is rather mild, he comes to YDC and is committed to a program for the emotionally disturbed as a result of aggressive behavior and as a result of sexual acting-out; they ask us to evaluate him.

My first concern is whether there is a history. I'm looking for a history of mental illness, a history of drug and alcohol abuse, and a history of criminal behavior. In this kid's case, his extended families also are positive for mental illness on both the mother's and father's sides, and includes both drug and alcohol abuse.

It could be any type of mental illness—could be depression, generalized anxiety disorder, bipolar disorder, schizophrenia, any mental illness.

There's predictive value for problems such as depression and attention deficit hyperactivity disorder. And naturally we are well aware of the biological predisposition for addiction. This person initially was diagnosed with recurrent severe major depression, without psychotic features, learning disability and arrested development, and pervasive developmental disorder. Very obese, anxious, and a history of heart murmur.

The psychosocial factors that are important in looking at this really have to do with abandonment—no contact with father, placements, frequent changes in schools, and ongoing psychiatric and behavior problems. Also, multiple diagnosis was diagnosed after that with Asperger syndrome, bipolar disorder, ADHD [attention deficit/hyperactivity disorder], and oppositional disorder. Most recently, when he came to our facility, our consulting psychiatrists basically saw him with dysthymic disorder, attention deficit/hyperactivity disorder, and generalized anxiety disorder. So now we have all this going on, and they ask us to do an evaluation, and we do that.

So he was interviewed by me and a staff psychologist who works for me. By the way, this kid was maintained on 500 mg of Depakote and also Adderall at the time of testing. He was rather unkempt, overweight, periods of fidgeting, moving around in the chair shaking his legs, affect relatively flat, very restricted, and a long history of suicide attempts, although he denied this at the time. I focused my inquiry at that time on his sexual history, because this is what we're looking at. He talked about learning about sex when he was five years old.

He was actually molested by a couple of female neighbors, but most of his acting out behavior was in institutions; he was in and out of institutions. He basically acted out sexually with other boys.

He did act out sexually in the community. He didn't say whether it was male or female. He was frequently neglected and exposed to high-risk situations. He believes he was molested by his parents when he was a little baby; however, he didn't have a personal recollection of that. That's something we just talked about.

He said he learned masturbatory behavior in placement. He said that he would frequently get involved with kids, and they would have group types of masturbation. He denied any previous intercourse with a female—strictly males.

He was also a victim of violence. He was threatened with violence and raped. He was victimized in two other placements by other adolescents. He was also physically abused in his family.

The mother and father relationship—the father wasn't there, he was completely absent, and the mother was an addict. He says he was exposed to high-risk situations. One can assume, knowing addiction, with the people coming in and out of the house, that he was exposed to a chaotic environment.

When he came to us, the first thing is we know he's a severe threat to act out sexually. What he did in placement was learn to associate violence with sex. He was exposed to these behaviors; impulsive young boys in placement would make comments. He admits to rape fantasies. He also admitted to frequent thoughts about rape fantasies. He began to verbalize threats of rape toward the African-American female staff when he was down there.

Now what happens with him is that we do the evaluation and identify these problems. We use everything from MMPI to projective drawings; I'm not going to get into details of all these, but there are significant mental health problems. What this all shakes down to is that we have the Abel assessment for sexual interest being positive for preschool females, grade-school females, adolescent females, preschool males, grade-school males, adolescent males, and adult males. Then there's reported self-arousal to preschool boys, grade-school boys. So we have visual reaction time (VRT) scores that are very positive.

We started with diagnostically. Diagnostically we see him as conduct disorder, adolescent onset. Type: attention deficit/hyperactivity disorder. Dysthymic disorder is very frequent in terms of criminal behavior with paraphilias, you see a lot of learning disorders, and we diagnose him on Axis 2 with Pervasive Developmental Disorder—NOS by history. Now, what do we want to do with him? We know that the kid is sexually inappropriate toward staff— we know there's danger toward staff. We also know that he has a history of perpetrating against young males, and that he has deviant sexual interests by his own admission. So he's not hiding anything. Basically it all gets progressively more and more out of control. So what we do here, we say, relative to his inappropriateness with objective findings related to sustained sexual interests in children, we say that this kid needs a specific protocol of treatment—sex-offense-specific treatment.

He is in an environment in which he is comfortable, and he finds it very stimulating. What he's learned to do is have intercourse and sexually act out with males in placement.

It continues as he gets out into the community. So he's learned this is the place! So here's your main approach to a kid like this. First, you have to appreciate the fact that the person has a mental illness—he's mentally ill. You have to educate him about his mental illness, and you have to assist him in becoming stable. Because what's going to happen is the depression will exacerbate the sexual acting out. Second, we know that the kid has been dysthymic for a lot of years, we know he has a history of sexual abuse, so we are going to hypothesize that when this kid begins to feel bad about himself and more and more depressed, then people are more and more at risk. So we need to make sure that we stabilize him and that's gone through individual and group cognitive behavioral therapy, that's also done pharmacologically—specific to mental health issues. Thus, we have a person with multiple paraphilias. So now this person has to be exposed to a protocol of treatment that will address his deviant sexual urges and deviant fantasies as necessary to prevent sexual re-offending. He has to address the issues related to emotional and sexual self-regulation.

Now, there is an OCD [obsessive compulsive disorder] spectrum that a lot of people believe some of the paraphiliacs fit into. That means a differentiation does have to be made, because a differentiation really has some implication for treatment.

You know, there's a big difference between a pathological presentation of OCD and a preoccupation with something. That has to be differentiated, and there's a lot of people who are preoccupied with having sex who are not OCD.

So, that gets a little tricky, and we try the best we can to discriminate, but the vast majority of what I see is not an OCD-driven kind of thing. You have to insist on looking at their past trauma, sexual offending, and past victimization, as re-offense potential. So what you're doing, you're not really beaming in on them as a victim, but you're taking a look at their own victimization.

You want to reduce as much as possible the inappropriate urges, fantasies, and behaviors, while simultaneously accelerating age-appropriate sexual fantasies and behaviors. That's the object. Not to make them asexual, but to get them more age-appropriate. And there's a number of other things. You teach them the sexual assault cycle. That has to be done so they understand exactly what goes on with them and how they become more and more out of control.

We use a monitoring system that a resident fills out every day regarding inappropriate sexual urges, fantasies and behaviors, as well as appropriate sexual urges, the Sexual Arousal Monitoring System (SAMS) developed at New Castle YDC. The youth then talks about them and we have a list of fantasies, targets, that we check off, and then the behaviors. The sexual behaviors, whether they masturbate, touch themselves, watching or staring while they're grooming, all these types of things. We also use a sexual distress index, as I call it, which addresses control and urge. And what they'll do is they'll go from one to five, one being no control and five being the most control. And they will estimate their level of urges that day, and hence their level of control.

We want to decelerate interest in deviant sexual behavior and at the same time increase age-appropriate sexual interest. Comprehensive sexual education is also necessary, emphasizing normal adolescent development. That's imperative.

You have to be teaching people what is normal, and then, skills building. Now you have the other side—you have sex-offense-specific assessments and treatment. Now, what you have to do is you also have to understand there's another side to this, and that's the social skills building, such as self-esteem, social problem-solving skills, relationship enhancement, intimacy training, sexual education, anger management, assertiveness training, adolescent refusal skills.

We want to stay away from a deficit model that is punishment oriented. The deficit model, what it really does is look at the kid's weaknesses. The deficit model looks at the weakness and says, "Don't do this, don't do that, don't do this, don't do that, and when this or that happens, block this, block that," and so forth. Well, you're doing two things here, you want to decelerate, but at the same time, you need to give somebody tools. This person knew how to talk to somebody, but he didn't know anything about dating or relationships or intimacy, and so on. If he did, there's a chance that this person might be behaving differently.

We use both group sessions and educational group sessions. It's imperative that this person is cognizant of mental health needs. Its process should be to focus on understanding the relationship between being dysregulated affectively, sexual offenses, and re-offense behavior. He requires ongoing treatment utilizing cognitive behavioral therapy to address mental health symptoms. You have got the traditional sexual offender therapy. If the non-pharmacological method is unsuccessful in reducing deviant urges and fantasy behavior, a trial of SSRIs should be considered.

See where we went there? We're going to go here, then we're going to go to the trial of SSRI, and then we talk a little bit about learning disabilities, etc.

Now, in this case here, the next step then would be that if this person didn't respond to various SSRIs, several different SSRIs should be tried when treatment failure occurs. The next step would be to convene a meeting and look at the possibility of doing anti-androgen therapy. Discuss its benefits. You have to understand there's a lot of issues in and around young people in terms of bone density, etc. There's a lot of lab work that has to be done. The person has to be medically cleared, and the biggest thing to understand is it is not FDA-approved treatment for sex offenders. That's the main thing. This is used very prudently to reduce sexual libido. It does that.

There are people who are advocates of Depo and other people who are advocates of oral therapy; it just depends. In this agency and facility we don't use Depo. When anti-androgen therapy is decided, we use oral administration. And that's really the safety feature. So we can control, God forbid, if something happens, because those shots might be once a month or once every two weeks. So it's really a big-time safety issue. Along with anti-androgen therapy, we use SAMS Forms to monitor treatment response as well as close medical supervision of side effects, blood levels, lab work. The SAMS Forms were developed by a supervisor in the sex offenders program and myself.

Relative to the aforestated information, the prognosis for this resident is considered poor. A most likely post-institutional placement would consider a Community Living Arrangement (CLA) through mental health. A comprehensive individual safety plan, pharmacotherapy, and ongoing talk therapy would be considered necessary for continuity of care.

Acknowledgments: We would like to acknowledge Charlie Chervanik and Joan Lawer of the PA Dept. of Public Welfare; the Office of Children, Youth, and Family Services; and Bob Liggett and Elida Evans at YDC-NC for supporting and financing significant amounts of specialized education, training, and certification in sexual offender evaluation, treatment, and risk predictions.

Critical Thinking Questions

1. **What issues would you personally have about being a sex offender therapist?**

2. **Would you want to get involved in this field? Why or why not?**

3. **Do you agree with the community living arrangement recommendation for this youth after release?**

PATRICIA J. LUTZ, MED, CETD: FOUNDER AND DIRECTOR, THE TURNING POINT, WASHINGTON, PENNSYLVANIA

We get a few girls and women directly from jails. For example, when certain girls get arrested, their probation officer may contact us for a possible placement and then bring them to us directly from jail. Most of our clients, however, have been in some kind of in-patient program prior to coming to this type of living situation. In other cases, the courts will refer the girls directly to us and, in yet other cases, the courts will mandate that a girl go into a rehabilitation program and then to us. Some young women may have insurance to pay for the services they receive, whereas probation officers will work with others to get welfare support for our program.

The girls usually have a long history of problems, and some begin to get into trouble as early as the eighth grade. Some have gone to Abraxis, an in-patient program for adolescents with drug and alcohol problems. Others may have gone to other out-patient programs, or they may start in an out-patient program as a result of a referral by their high school counselor.

Our program is for girls eighteen years and older. We don't have an adolescent program, but the history of the girls we get often starts back in the seventh or eighth grades. A lot of their history begins with retail theft. One of our young women who as a young girl lived in Mt. Lebanon, an upper-class area of Pittsburgh, relates sneaking out of her house, going down to Kaufman's Department Store, and stealing jewelry.

The first addiction often is nicotine. The girls will start by stealing and smoking cigarettes and then, if their parents or grandparents happen to be on some kind of medication, the girls will be drawn to that and start stealing and using that drug. A lot of them, if they are invited to your home, for instance, will go through your medicine cabinet. They can get away with it because most people don't count the pills in the medicine bottles they receive from pharmacists. So they start taking some medicine from their parents or their grandparents, especially if the medicine is some type of pain medication; the kids, however, will try anything.

When I think about the history of working people I've dealt with over the years, it's oftentimes the youngest rather than the oldest child in the family who gets involved in the drugs—at least that's my sense of it. I don't know why that is, unless perhaps the parents have less time for the youngest child as the family matures. There would be more time for parental direction with only one child in the family. However, situations vary. One girl with three older brothers and a sister said her mother was addicted to the telephone. When the youth fell and broke her elbow, the kids came in the house to say, "Mom, mom, Betty broke her arm." And the mother is on the phone telling them to stay out and be quiet because she's on the phone.

The progression then turns to retail theft. The child is incorrigible, starts to act out in and miss school, and may be referred to a place like Abraxis, or some other special program. The lucky ones graduate, but most of them are very intelligent. They are not in special education classes and are very, very bright. They try to figure out how to get over on whatever the system is, including this facility, and I think that is an important clue.

There is a kind of addiction to the chaos and excitement of getting over on someone or something. I think that produces an adrenaline rush for them, the same as getting high on a drug or engaging in retail theft. There is the high, a holding of the breath, and an exhilaration that comes with those behaviors; it is in their body, their body structure, their muscles, and what's going on with them biophysically. I think that's really what they're addicted to.

Then, as the drug addiction increases, they need more money and have to spend more time getting their drugs. In fact, yesterday a girl said getting drugs and getting high was an all-day affair. So, she's bored, because it takes all day, from whenever she wakes up at 3 o'clock in the afternoon until whenever she goes to sleep at three o'clock in the morning. It takes a lot of time just to get the money and score the drug. They then figure that they have to steal bigger items, and they move into more serious "boosts." They start shoplifting expensive items like TV or stereo sets from Wal-Mart and other places—the largest items that they can carry out of the store and re-sell—and now they are into serious felonies. They may start robbing houses, and many times I hear them say, "Well, I was in the car waiting. I didn't know that they were going to rob that house." But that's the type of progression they go through.

As their need for more drugs grows, so does their need for different drugs. This appears to be because they are now playing a game of more, better, and different: "I want it more, I want it better, and I want it different." And that continues to grow. So then they get into some more serious crimes like armed robbery. The scenario is the same as that of a guy. That is, the girls get a real or a fake gun, or a knife, and go into a store, and take the money, and leave.

Some girls can get pretty violent, but more often they are the victims of violence. I've had some girls who have been shot dealing drugs; women aren't so much shooters as the victims of being shot. I had one girl who had her finger cut off because of a bad drug deal. I've had women knifed, and I have had girls who have knifed other people. It's probably safe to say that women are more likely to knife you than shoot you.

I did have a woman in residence here who actually would threaten to knife us, but I always called her bluff because I didn't think she would ever actually hurt anyone here. She was just blowing hot air and taking a "tough-ass" attitude. She might have knifed somebody while she was under the influence, and she did have a history of stabbing, but I think once she moved into the "normal" world, the threat was no more than just a threat or an attempt to act tough. It wasn't an action that she would have taken. Simply put, living on the streets was threatening, so she carried a knife and she developed a reputation of being crazy with this knife, so people would stay away from her and the drug dealers would accommodate her. The reason I was not worried about her knifing someone here is because once you get the chemicals out of your system, you're able to settle down into some sort of stable lifestyle. I believed she was settling down.

In other words, at heart, I don't believe that these people are serious criminals. Most of the felonies that they have are due to the drug addiction, but once they get beyond that, they are not felons. They should not be in Muncie, a maximum-security facility, but many of our girls do some time in Muncie if they commit enough serious offenses.

Another problem is that in addition to drugs and alcohol, some of the girls have co-occurring mental health issues such as bipolar disorder, borderline personality disorder, conduct disorder, and depression. We try to get them maintained on some kind of medicine, but that is a big problem because the girls still need that fix from their restlessness, their irritability, and their discontentment, and treatment takes time. But, if they are willing to put the time into their rehab, the need for the fix is going to get less as the months and the years go by. But, too often, people are in a hurry to get better. They don't like the anxiety they still experience early in recovery. A lot of those physical symptoms do not disappear, and they must deal with those symptoms throughout their whole recovery, perhaps for years. So we've had people who are clean and sober for ninety days and then shoplift because they want that rush or fix from doing something and getting away with it. If we discover they have shoplifted something, they have to march right back down to the store and return the item.

Another problem the girls have is that, without their drug of choice, they have mood swings. Many of them are still addicted to relationships, sex, or the chase to get the relationship. So they look for excitement. Many give up one addiction and look for something else that will give them the same kind of feeling. It could be shoplifting, it could be men, it could be work for some; in fact, some become workaholics. They'll move onto something else that gives them that sense of well-being that they're seeking.

In addition, many of the girls come to us on medication, but sometimes not the right medication, so we have a psychiatrist evaluate them as they're going through the program. Realistically, I think that finding the right medication is almost a crapshoot. The psychiatrists have to really work with a girl to see what works, because each person is different. But let's say a girl hasn't been medicated yet and, after about thirty to sixty days of sobriety, is still experiencing mood swings, angry outbursts, and many ups and downs throughout the day. We will then have a psychiatric evaluation done so that the doctor is able to prescribe the proper medication for that person. Now, the patient might have to take medication all of her life in addition to staying sober.

After a while, another problem pops up. Patients tell themselves, "Well, I've been sober now for four years and my life is working OK, so I'm going to stop the medicine." Then, they get right back in trouble because as soon as they stop the medicine, all the psychiatric symptoms come back, and they try to self-medicate with alcohol and drugs. The cycle begins all over again. It's hard for the women to realize that they must work with multiple medical problems simultaneously.

This process raises issues of normalcy for these women. I tell them that if they are taking their medicine and not drinking or doing drugs, then they are as close to normal as they are ever going to get. Most of these women want desperately to be normal; that is, they really long to be what they *think* is normal. And I ask them, number one, "What is normal?" And then, number two, I tell them, "This is as close as you're going to get to normal." Normal for me is very broad, and I need to get them to understand that taking medicine and fighting their emotions and ways of thinking is normal for them.

An important key to the girls making it is to convince them that, if they continue their lifestyle, they will die. These young girls already are having enormous gynecological problems, and I think that's where the change begins to come from—they can be convinced that if they do one more run, if they get one more arrest, then they are going to die. That's what motivates them more than anything else, but it is very difficult for nineteen-year-olds to accept that they can never use drugs or alcohol again. Once they realize that they can die from the drugs or alcohol, or the complications of their use, or from hepatitis C, or HIV, and their complications, they have a chance, but it's not easy.

They have to take it one day at a time. The decision can be made at an early age, but it has to be a short, short idea, such as, "I'm only going to do it today." Then, the next day, they have to say the same thing again. Eventually, they can string those days together and experience years of sobriety.

Sadly, some people cannot or will not put out the effort. They're here just for a rest. They're really here just to get off the streets for six months or so and then go back to the streets. In fact, we just had a girl leave who was doing extremely well and ready to get her apartment, but she left and went back to the streets; she is now back on drugs and alcohol. Others might be sober for twenty years and do the same thing. A partial solution requires them to be sick and tired of being sick and tired.

Interviewed in June 2006.

Critical Thinking Questions

1. **Can you think of any other steps or experiences that young girls might have that would aid their progression into drugs and alcohol?**

2. **Once a young female begins her progression into drugs and alcohol, in what other types of behaviors might she get engaged?**

3. **Explain what the "rush" is and its dynamics.**

4. **As a therapist, what would you do to help an offender understand the "rush"?**

5. **Describe what a "support system" might look like for one of the offenders described above.**

6. **What appear to be the "mood dynamics" that these girls go through? Explain the complexities of these dynamics.**

PETER REINHARZ, FORMER CHIEF OF THE NEW YORK CITY LAW DEPARTMENT FOR THE FAMILY COURT DIVISION

I was the Chief Prosecutor of the New York City Family Court Division, which meant that I was in charge of the prosecution of juvenile crime.

In New York City, the Family Court deals with juvenile crime. For juvenile crime, the first role of probation is as an arm of the court, even though the court is a state court in New York; the probation department is a city department. Probation serves as an intake facility that receives the cases from the police department following an arrest. The probation department then determines whether or not to adjust the case; that is, deal with the case through an immediate referral to the different services available, or to refer the case for prosecution.

The people who make these decisions are probation officers with some background in the social sciences who are assigned to make these decisions and others who work as supervisors; these officers all have specialized training.

When a case comes into probation there usually are conferences with the kid and his family. One of the things that has to happen in order to get a successful adjustment is that the parent actually has to agree. The protocol is that the parent has to participate, because if the parent is not involved, obviously the chance of a successful adjustment is limited.

Every juvenile is evaluated. The school records are sought, and if the kid has a prior record and considerable activity, then obviously the chances of adjustment are diminished. So probation will make an initial assessment, but the final assessment as to whether or not probation is going to refer the case doesn't have to take place for a period of up to sixty days.

During the assessment, the department, first of all, of course, looks at the gravity of the offense. The assessment also helps the department determine whether or not the kid is amenable to any sort of treatment or program, and whether or not the family is cooperating. If the family is cooperating, the youth will be sent to a program that can work with the youth's needs.

Even if the department decides to refer the youth to the juvenile court, section 326.1 of the Family Court Act allows for a referral back to probation at the arraignment, which is sometimes "prejudicial appearance" in statute. The court or prosecution can turn and say, "Let's give this case back to probation and see whether or not they can actually adjust it." An officer from probation will come in, and we will say, "Let's give it another shot."

Before we refer it, though, if a victim were involved, we would contact the victim to see whether the victim is agreeable to adjustment. So we talk to the victim and also probably get information from the kid's lawyer that could sway us to forgo prosecution in favor of an adjustment. The lawyer, for example, may convince us that this is really an isolated incident, that this kid is very amenable, and that this kid shows a certain amount of remorse. Obviously, a display of remorse is very important, because someone accepting the responsibility for their behavior is really the key to showing that the kid is on his way to staying out of trouble.

As a prosecutor, then, I would turn, case back over to probation because they are the people most involved with the kid. For example, in some situations we may see that the kid is involved in some sort of destructive behavior or we may see something that tells us that he would be better off in X program or Y program.

It is unlikely, but if fires or matches were involved, only an outside chance exists that we might refer it down. In reality, though, if fire and matches were involved, it is unlikely we would refer it down for adjustment services.

Robberies would not be referred down; robbery is a felony. With a robbery, we are not talking some sort of adjustment. But, if we are dealing with some sort of a minor theft—let's say, for example, that the theft involved someone joy riding in a neighbor's car and the plaintiff and the kid knew each other—then we might be amenable to referring the case down. Obviously, the car could not be damaged. If it seems like it is an isolated incident and is unlikely to repeat itself, then we would talk to the victim and ask, "Is this kid out of control in the neighborhood?" And if they were to say, "No, I've never seen this from the kid before," then we might not prosecute this particular boy. If everybody, including the plaintiff, is willing, we would very likely just leave it alone, and say, "OK send it back to probation."

When you start talking about fights, then we look at it much more carefully. Property damage and personal injury are two are very different things. The advantage of going with a full prosecution is that we are still dealing with the juvenile criminal case, and a juvenile prosecution is not something that is going to burden a kid with a criminal record forever. We understand that and that is the advantage of the juvenile system.

If adjudication takes place, a full workup will be done on the kid. That means probation will do what they call an "I and R," an Investigation and Report. Some sort of mental health study will be conducted by a psychiatrist or psychologist that will be very extensive, particularly if the youth is involved in assaultive behavior, and when placement is considered an option. On the other hand, if it were the kind of assault where somebody was aggressive when they should not have been aggressive, and if there is any sort of indication of a history of either violence or anger, then we are not sending that kid back down. Nobody is going to trust that kid.

If, on the other hand, the assault is a misdemeanor assault, like a schoolyard fight, and the kid has no record, we very likely would send it down, but that case probably would not come to us in the first place.

There are also less serious cases that we call PINS (Persons in Need of Supervision) cases, whereas other jurisdictions call them CHINS (Children in Need of Supervision). Since our office is a prosecutors' office, we only deal with crime; probation would handle the PINS cases, and in New York it is now mandatory to divert or adjust those cases. It is almost impossible to get those cases into court. So the status offenders, the kids who are out of control, the runaways and cases like those must go through the adjustment process—It is mandatory.

An interesting area of our concern is prostitution, and I have often taken a tough stance on prostitution. The reason is simple, because I believe that the girls, and in some cases the boys, who are involved with selling themselves really need to be separated from the streets by force. Before I left in 2002, we were working on a case against a number of pimps. In these cases, we were working on both the juvenile and adult sides. For example, gangs were involved in taking girls as young as ten years of age and putting them out on the street.

Initially, we would put the girls into shelters or non-secure facilities. The pimps would walk right into these facilities and just take them out. So I advocated for the secure detention of these kids. Some people thought is it was too harsh to detain prostitutes securely but I said no—because the kids either runaway from the facilities or the pimps come in and get them. Frankly, we need a certain period of time, be it a week or ten days, just to get the kids straightened out or deprogrammed and back with their families. The Bloods [gang] are especially troublesome here. The Bloods are probably the biggest organized crime prostitution service in New York, and they control tremendous numbers of prostitutes in the city.

New York City has an agency called the Department of Juvenile Justice that runs the secure detention facilities. I most often advocated placing the kids [involved in prostitution] in secure detention really to protect them from themselves, to keep them away from the gang element that was coming in.

Drug cases are also handled in different ways. It is very rare for a first-time drug offender to get detention for selling drugs; it is possible, but they probably would be in non-secure detention depending upon the type of drug (such as marijuana) and what happened in the case. The second time a kid comes in, it is possible that he could wind up in detention, either secure or not secure, depending on what happened on the first case.

If, however, the first contact for the drugs was for really heavy duty offending, an A and B felony, for example, we detained, or at least sought detention, as a general rule. But if the kid comes in with all sorts of indicators for detention, and the parent comes in and says, "Look, I haven't seen the kid in three weeks. Can't I just take him home?" for a P.L. §220.3, which is a misdemeanor drug case with small amount of drug for personal use, or minor selling of something like marijuana, the youth would very likely wind up going home and be supervised by the probation department.

For more serious sale and distribution involvement, the youths would not be sent back down, simply because kids who sell and distribute narcotics or hallucinogens like PCP usually are hooked up a little higher in the chain in the neighborhood. We do our best to make sure they get away from those higher-ups. One of the things that the juvenile justice system *can* do is separate kids from the associations that they have—and that is important. When kids get separated from the negative influences, sometimes they go back to being kids again.

Gangs are yet another story and are always a funny sort of thing. One of the first things you learn when dealing with kids is that those who display the gang behavior and talk tough, when you arrest them are the "wannabes." Then, you see kids with temporary tattoos of a particular gang—but they scratch off—a d you say, "What's that?", and they say, "Oh yeah, I'm a Crip," or whatever it is. This kid needs to be protected from himself, because he is going to wind up getting himself shot. This youth is more of a gang wannabe than an actual gang member.

Real gang members will not necessarily admit their affiliation in the beginning, so you have to look for different indicators. You look at a fifteen-year-old with certain tattoos and you say, "What's that?", and he says, "That's nothing." That is an indicator that Johnny is deep into the gang culture, and that is a little scary.

These problems are rampant throughout the schools. New York City schools vary from some of the best in the nation to some of the worst. Some of these schools are affected badly by the violence within and around their hallways. We have to stay in tune with this, because the bulk of the kids in these schools are going there every day because they want to learn; they do not need to be afraid to go to the bathroom or walk the halls.

As a prosecutor you have to realize, this is not just a social problem of turning a kid around, but a criminal justice problem too. The point is that people get hurt and are victims. In addition, the adult crime rate is affected by juvenile crime. If you look at the UCRs, boys age thirteen really are starting to get into violent crimes and are very dangerous at age eighteen, nineteen, and twenty, but they may not be dangerous in another seven, eight, or maybe nine, years. The systems that exist right now do not really focus on that.

The systems are geared towards giving the kid who makes a mistake another chance. The important thing for the system is to isolate the kids who are making youthful errors from kids who are predatory. It is a responsibility of the juvenile justice system, just like the adult system, to isolate the predators. That is my philosophy.

The New York statute gives you the grounds for detaining people, and we use that as often as necessary. Now, there are different philosophies out there and different views even among prosecutors as to when somebody needs and does not need to be detained. A deflection from the system can be a good thing for the offender if the offender is amenable to treatment. Also, keeping kids out of detention is really great rhetoric for people who want to avoid incarcerating these kids. But the problem is that some kids are predatory and hurting people; that is not good.

The Prosecutor's office itself does not have programs for these offenders. The Probation Department and the Office of Children and Youth Services, however, have anti-gang and other programs to which youths can be referred after adjudication, and we sometimes refer youths back and forth to one another. For example, if Johnny Jones is a known gang member and admits that he is already in the adult system, and his little brother comes in very early, we might flag that case and intervene with the youth aggressively. But it is very difficult to know what kind of success you might have in the really hard gang cases.

The juvenile justice system, in my view, has everything backwards. As I said before, crime really tends to escalate by age thirteen. The "Return to Prison" programs say that teenagers are the most likely to go back. The idea of giving teens and twenty-year-olds a juvenile or youthful offender status—the shortest prison terms for the most predatory kids—is not a good idea. These kids need to be isolated for a longer period of time.

Then, you have the other side of the coin. You have the people who say three strikes and you are out. You get the kid who is seventeen or eighteen who is a really violent person. At seventeen he gets arrested once, at eighteen he gets arrested again, and at nineteen is arrested for the third time, and we say, " OK, put him away for life." That is also stupid because by the time that guy is thirty-five and a lifer, he is probably not a danger to anyone. I mean, there are people in their forties who are dangerous but, to tell you the truth, most of us know that as people get older they tend to avoid violence. A sense of mortality seems to overtake most of us around age twenty-three, twenty-four, or twenty-five. Once that sinks in, we start to calm down a bit. The offenders who are very dangerous at age eighteen, nineteen, and twenty may not be dangerous in another seven, eight, or maybe nine, years. So there really has to be something in the system that would allow kids to still maintain juvenile status and not ruin their whole lives by being in prison.

Personally, I would set up a system that takes the really violent kids and isolates them for a long period of time. I would school them, even if it means holding them for significant periods of time, even providing them with college courses while they are there until they actually reach an age, very likely somewhere in their mid twenties, when they are no longer dangerous. Then we would evaluate them and say, "Well, you are probably ready for release now." And I would let them out knowing that they did not have a felony record, that their juvenile record was protected, and that they could probably move on with their life having calmed down.

Mr. Reinharz is currently the Managing Attorney of County Attorney's Office of Nassau County, New York, and today does not deal with juvenile crimes. Please note that the views herein are Mr. Reinharz's and, while they may have been a part of his former office's program, may not necessarily reflect the present position of the City of New York. Mr. Reinharz was interviewed in June 2006.

Critical Thinking Questions

1. **How does this view of a juvenile prosecutor compare with your view of juvenile prosecutors?**

2. **What are the various options open to juvenile prosecutors, and under what conditions do those options become available?**

3. **This prosecutor believes that some youths are kept in confinement far too long. What is your impression of the reasons behind his opinion? Is his opinion reasonable, in your point of view?**

PATRICIA BRENNAN, DEPUTY COMMISSIONER OF PROBATION, NEW YORK CITY

I started with the department of probation in 1972 and stayed with the department for fifteen years before moving on to several other government positions. Initially I was a family court probation officer and served as an Investigation PO. I did supervision, some special projects working within our alternative-to-detention program, and then, for the last three years that I was in the department, I was in special projects, special operations review team, and executive assistant to one of the deputy commissioners.

At that time, the department of probation did in fact deal with the status offender (PINS) as well as juvenile delinquents.

Let's start with the PINS. On an annual basis, New York City was seeing anywhere between 5,000 and 6,000 status offenders. After many years of public debate, legislators were persuaded that these non-criminal, acting-out juveniles were receiving unfair, inconsistent, or ineffective interventions. So, in 1985, New York State passed the PINS Adjustment Services Act. There was a period of planning, and in 1987, PINS Diversion was implemented in NYC. The legislation was based on the conviction that many cases involving PINS could be resolved through non-judicial remedies, with much more success for the youth and the family. The major goals of diversion included better meeting the needs of troubled children and their families, helping to keep families together by reducing out-of-home placements, and reducing unnecessary or inappropriate use of the court. The legislation also called for local jurisdictions to create an interagency planning process to encourage collaboration among relevant local and State agencies. Incentive funding was provided to set up planning groups and figure out how better to identify, assess, and provide services to the PINS child. This really was the start of changing our practice, which has continued to evolve further over the last twenty years.

A typical remark that might be made then was that there is a juvenile justice system, "Like it or not, there is a system." But a PINS system simply did not exist, and there were so many misconceptions and misunderstandings about how status offenders should be handled that families and even professionals believed that they needed to go to court to get services for this specialized group.

The plan did not exclude juveniles from going to court entirely, but the idea was that if you offered community based services to a family and a youth in crisis, you could avert a lot of the delays that come as a result of entering a legal arena. After all, court procedures are generally adversarial in nature. I think diversion was the right way to go. Imagine for a moment that you have a child and a parent who are at odds with each other. You throw them into the legal arena where each of them gets an attorney, and they sit on opposite sides of the room and hurl allegations at each other. Then the judge adjourns the case and they're supposed to go home together. This process will likely not improve the child's behavior, nor increase the parent's authority and effectiveness. But the idea behind diversion was to de-escalate the crisis and help the families.

The right amount of implementation money was dedicated to the services, and the plan worked reasonably well for about ten years. Then, it began to break down.

The legislation defined the role for probation. Our role was, and this is a quote, to determine "eligibility and suitability" of the potential PINS respondent for diversion services. The legislation largely revolved around getting both the child and the parent to accept diversion services. In fact, I will tell you, that outside of the youth having an open delinquency matter such as outstanding warrants from the court or a prior out-of-home placement, exclusions were pretty narrowly defined. Once the department got the parents and child to agree, obtained the agreement, and got some basic case information, the youth's PO (case manager) referred the case to the borough/county Designated Assessment Services (DAS) that then assessed the youth and family and referred them to community service programs.

The probation officers did not themselves engage in counseling during this process, which was a change within our Intake function. Their primary purpose was to explain the PINS process to the parties and to obtain the agreement of the parents and children to accept the services and referral to the assessment unit. Did they pound out a mediation document? Did they pound out all that was going to happen, for example, that a curfew was going to be set? No, they did not. The specifics were left to the Designated Assessment Services.

To address the issue of counseling a little further—in the pre-PINS Diversion days, we had staff who were literally running groups for kids who were diverted; we had trained them for that skill level. Today, I do not think that staff have that skill level. I would not compare every single one of my POs with an MSW who might be doing counseling in a community agency. I think we have to know what our limits are, and if it is a type of counseling that can substantiate and reinforce what is being done out in the community, then I can say, "Yes, that is what we do." I think most PO's have a certain skill level with regard to that kind of counseling. Additionally, we were underfunded for staff, so it quickly became obvious that we had to scale back our role. With only sixteen POs citywide, it was impossible for us to perform the same in-depth work with 5 – 6,000 PINS.

In the initial fact-gathering, a probation officer has to be a skilled interviewer. But, the officer might be pushed to do some counseling/crisis intervention because of people's expectation of, "Well, if I tell you the problem, then I want you to solve the problem." The PINS Adjustment Services Act spoke to this a little, because the act tried to downplay the level of involvement by all probation departments. In addition, the Designated Assessment Units also encouraged us to keep the interview to a respectable minimum. The reason was that you did not want a family in crisis to have to repeat its story two or three times in a day; that does not serve anyone well.

Again, the law was written in such a way that you could see its intent. The major thrust was that the youth was eligible and suitable as long as the youth and the parent agreed and that diversion programs had not been tried and failed again and again., The law was written in such a way that it really did intend that the vast majority of cases would be diverted.

Some PINS cases, of course, did get to court. Most of the court cases were of two types.

One was if the youth was missing from home and a warrant had been issued. The family had told the court, "My son or daughter has now left my domicile; I don't know where they are." Or, "I know where they are and I can't get them to leave there." Those cases would go to court because the youths were not, by definition, eligible or suitable since they had not been present at the intake appointment. The other type of case would be where there was absolutely no agreement between the youth and his or her parents. The parent: "No, I don't want services. I want to see the judge. I want the judge to send my child to a "boot camp." The youth: "No, I do not want to talk to anyone about this, I don't have a problem, this is all my mother or father's problem." These cases ended up in court at the request of the probation department.

The prosecutor had nothing to do with these PINS cases after; in fact prosecutors declined to be the presentment agency for the PINS population because they felt that there was a conflict of interest. As the prosecutor /presentment agency for juvenile delinquency cases, there were circumstances where they had "represented" a parent in a PINS petition where they would also be the prosecutor of that youth, their client's child as a delinquent) The judge might re-refer PINS cases to DOP for diversion , but historically, it was a very uneven process; for example, a youth represented by a Legal Aid Attorney would likely make a motion to the court to re-refer for diversion . The parents for the most part had no legal representation in court and their desires were "protected" and/or "inquired after" by the presiding judge.

The New York state legislature recently enacted yet other PINS legislation that has resulted in PINS cases being taken out of probation entirely in New York City. The New York State legislature told each jurisdiction that either the local probation department or the child welfare/social system should take over the PINS cases. New York City opted for a system that it actually had initiated informally several years before where the ACS (Administration for Children Services) had started to take responsibility for PINS cases. I think it was a smart idea, because ACS owned all the preventive services anyway. They funded the DAS units and the community-based programs anyway, so why work through a middle-man, which was exactly the unenviable position that probation was in prior to the passage of the new law.

Juvenile delinquency cases also get to the juvenile court, but again, depending upon a number of factors. Once again, we have guidelines, and the law is fairly generous in the discretion that it gives the Department of Probation. The police bring all juveniles cases within the jurisdiction of the family court to juvenile probation. The DOP does not make decisions on the basis of legal sufficiency only the prosecutor, who declines approximately 30 percent of the cases brought in, does that. If there is legal insufficiency, they decline. If it is a case that they do not want to prosecute as they feel it is better dealt with by offering diversion services, they can and do re-refer to DOP.

For example, on just the merits of the arrest charge for designated very serious felonies— some fifteen categories—the law says that we cannot adjust without asking the court's permission. We do not, in other words, take a robbery in the second degree and adjust it. However, we do refer the case on to the court, present the facts about the youth arrested and his/her family, as well as point out any mitigating circumstances, and, even though it is a robbery two, if we felt diversion were appropriate, we would make it known. Beyond these limited exceptions, probation offices are, by statute, given fairly broad discretion regarding the charges.

You must not forget that the victim is a very important ingredient in all of this process and consideration as to diversion.

The law requires that the victim agree to divert from court. So it is not just the power and discretion that the probation officer has, but, in fact, whether the victim agrees to it. Imagine for a moment that this is a property crime and the victim says, "You know, given all the explanation about the process, I would be satisfied with the juvenile and his parents paying me for the damages. If they give me one hundred dollars, you can do whatever you want to do. I'll forget this matter and leave it in your hands."

In other words, the second half of this process is that if the victim says, "I want one hundred dollars, an apology, and two other conditions…", then we have to get an agreement from the parent and the juvenile that they can and will agree to reimburse or make restitution. So we have an agreement and a contract, but it revolves around the victim to some degree.

For example, if the victim is the same age as the juvenile perpetrator, our conversation is not just with the twelve-year-old, but also is with the parents of the victim. And there are lots of reasons why that parent might say, "You know, they used to be best friends, but they are not friends anymore, and I just don't want another fight to happen. I want this kid to stay away from my kid." So you talk to the adults in the situation and you find out what they want. It can be one youth taking license with an opportunity to bully someone or victimizing another youth who he or she doesn't know. In both cases, the victim and the victim's parents will be contacted.

Let's look at how some of the fifteen more serious types of cases that we must refer to the juvenile court might be handled. Much depends for both us and the victim on the youth's history. Was this the first time? Or was this the second or fifth time? We have authority to get information, so we find out, for example, how this youth is doing in school. If you call and speak with his guidance counselor, do you find out that the youth is in the guidance counselor's office every day? Probation Intake involves a very time-pressured mini-investigation where you are trying to find out the juvenile's strengths and weaknesses to determine how best to differentiate between those who can benefit from diversion and those who cannot. Keep in mind that our goal here is to have the greatest impact possible on the juvenile and to prevent future crimes from occurring.

The advantage that the Probation Department diversion has over the Juvenile Court process is that if a youth comes into our offices on any given day, we can immediately dispense a non-judicial sanction that day. We do not have to wait until six months from now when the court process has begun; court proceedings may drag out, depending on the intricacy of the case, the calendar of the court docket, and the way courts operate. This extended passage of time is not a good thing in a juvenile's life. I think swift and certain is the better way to be.

As we look at other delinquent offenses, we are very open for diversion on, for example, marijuana—especially the small amount where it appears to be for personal consumption only. And we have a fairly good number of substance, abuse programs that would be willing to work with a youth on that problem and report to us, and to drug-test the youth. As you go up the scale, you often are in collaboration with the prosecutor's office if you are talking PCP, ecstasy, or heroin, particularly with their sale. The youth here may be getting into serious stuff where, literally, they are not just using and not just selling, but are working for an organization that uses the younger kids for this purpose. Our reaction to that is, very justifiably, different from the easily identified marijuana user.

It is not a given that any particular drug case will go to the juvenile court and be prosecuted. It is possible that a youth getting involved in a gang and selling drugs might be put on diversion under very special circumstances, but the problem is whether the youth is more afraid of us or more afraid of the gang. The other aspect depends upon how the prosecutor wants to work with this. For example, sometimes the undercover cop may not want to lose his cover. So, depending upon the circumstances of the case and whether it is going to get prosecuted, we may get those cases back for diversion. We understand that the undercover cop and his role in this is more important than this particular case being prosecuted to its furthest level. So probation may get this youth back. The coordination of all of this can be quite hard, but it is the goal for DOP and the prosecutor's office to work closely together.

Probation has some institutional problems with the police as well. My Probation Department and the Family Court in New York City run Monday through Friday from 9 – 5. The police, on the other hand, operate 24/7; they can be on for the arrest and then off for three days. The statute says that my intake POs have seven days to accomplish a decision on the arrest, so they may expend days trying to get the arresting officer to call them back. Sometimes this is a problem. We may have to take it up the precinct chain of command, where we will attempt to speak to or get the desk sergeant to talk to us. Sometimes we are not able to reach the arresting officer as often as we like, which is unfortunate, as good information can be obtained from the arresting officer, both about the arrest and his or her experience with the youth in their community.

At the current time, we have an arrangement with the prosecutor's office that will help us in this area. It is not uncommon for the prosecutor's office to have a discussion with either the victim and/or arresting officer, who relay their preference not to pursue the matter at court level; a change of heart, perhaps, from when they spoke to DOP. We now identify cases where we had to refer the matter to the prosecutor, yet where we would be disposed to providing diversion services if it had not been for the victim's insistence at the time. It is not legislatively dictated; it is just good practice.

Ms. Brennan is a former probation officer in New York City and currently is Deputy Commissioner of Probation. Interviewed in July 2006, and printed with permission.

Critical Thinking Questions

1. **Before reading this interview, what was your view of a probation department and what it did?**

2. In what way(s) did the information in this interview change your perceptions of what you might expect your job to be if you became a probation officer?

3. Discuss the various options open to probation departments in dealing with their clients.